Project Staff

SUE DAVIDSON, *Editor*

MERLE FROSCHL, *Field-Testing Coordinator*

FLORENCE HOWE, *Director*

ELIZABETH PHILLIPS, *Editor*

SUSAN TROWBRIDGE, *Design and Production Director*

ALEXANDRA WEINBAUM, *Teaching Guide Editor*

Household and Kin

Families in Flux

Amy Swerdlow

Renate Bridenthal

Joan Kelly

Phyllis Vine

The Feminist Press

OLD WESTBURY, NEW YORK

The McGraw-Hill Book Company

NEW YORK, ST. LOUIS, SAN FRANCISCO

Cover Illustration by Ariane R. Berman
Photo Research by Flavia Rando

Library of Congress Cataloging in Publication Data

Main entry under title:
Household and kin.

  (Women's lives/women's work)
  Includes bibliographical references and index.
  1. Family—History. 2. Family—United States. I. Swerdlow, Amy. II. Series.
HQ503.H77   306.8'09   80-17038
ISBN 0-912670-91-6 (Feminist Press) ISBN 0-07-020427-6 pbk. (McGraw-Hill)
ISBN 0-912670-68-1 pbk. (Feminist Press)

The findings and conclusions of this volume do not necessarily represent the views of the National Endowment for the Humanities.

To the families we come from—
To the families we made—and—
To those who will make the future.

Table of Contents

xi   Publisher's Acknowledgments

xv   Authors' Acknowledgments

xvi   Introduction

1   **ONE: Family Life**
A Historical Perspective
By Joan Kelly

2   Kinds of Families
Kinship in Tribal Societies • Growing Up in Feudal Society • The Preindustrial Household

15   The Nuclear Family
Separating Work and Home • The Division of Family Labor • Women's Work in the Home

24   PHOTO FEATURE—Families Throughout History

33   Family and Sex Roles in Flux
Mother Has a Paying Job • A Longer and More Varied Life

47   **TWO: The Family Tree**
Contemporary Patterns in the United States
By Renate Bridenthal

47   What Is a Family?
Understanding Social Class • Who Is at Home?

68   Roots
Reaching for the "American Dream" • Getting By • The Wealthy and Powerful • People of Color • Sex Roles

76   PHOTO FEATURE—Today's Varied Families

90   Branches
Choosing to Marry • Choosing Not to Marry • Adoptive Families • Children in Institutions • The Last Difference

107 **THREE: The Search for Alternatives**

Past, Present, and Future
By Amy Swerdlow and Phyllis Vine

109 Models from the Past
Creating a Superior State • *The Pursuit of
Happiness* • *Reorganizing the Private Home* •
Scientific Socialism • *The Kibbutz*

128 PHOTO FEATURE—Alternative Family Patterns

131 The Nuclear Household Transformed
The Cuban Family Code • *Family Policy in Sweden* •
Shared Parenting in the United States

146 Contemporary Communal Families
The Circle of Families • *Counterculture Communes*

157 The Future for All of Us

161 About the Authors
163 Notes
173 Index
181 A Note on Language

Publisher's Acknowledgments

EARLY IN 1973, Mariam Chamberlain and Terry Saario of the Ford Foundation spent one day visiting The Feminist Press on the campus of the State University of New York, College at Old Westbury. They heard staff members describe the early history of The Feminist Press and its goal—to change the sexist education of girls and boys, women and men, through publishing and other projects. They also heard about those books and projects then in progress; they felt our sense of frustration about how little we were able to do directly for the classroom teacher. Advising us about funding, Terry Saario was provocative. "You need to think of yourselves," she said, "in the manner of language labs, testing and developing new texts for students and new instructional materials for teachers." Our "language" was feminism, our intent to provide alternatives to the sexist texts used in schools. The conception was, in fact, precisely the one on which the Press had been founded.

Out of that 1973 meeting came the idea for the *Women's Lives / Women's Work* project. This project, which would not officially begin for more than two years, has allowed us to extend the original concept of The Feminist Press to a broader audience.

We spent the years from 1973 to 1975 assessing the need for a publication project, writing a major funding proposal, steering it through two foundations, negotiating with the Webster Division of McGraw-Hill, our co-publisher. We could not have begun this process without the advice and encouragement of Marilyn Levy of the Rockefeller Family Fund, from which we received a planning grant in 1973. For one year, Phyllis Arlow, Marj Britt, Merle Froschl, and Florence Howe surveyed the needs of teachers for books about women, reviewed the sexist bias of widely used history and literature texts, and interviewed editorial staffs of major educational publishers about their intentions to publish material on women. The research accumulated provided a strong case for the grant proposal first submitted to the Ford Foundation in the summer of 1974.

During the winter of 1974–75, Merle Froschl, Florence Howe, Corrine Lucido, and attorney Janice Goodman (for The Feminist Press) negotiated a co-publishing contract with McGraw-Hill. We could not have proceeded without the strong interest of John Rothermich of McGraw-Hill's Webster Division. Our co-publishing agreement gives control over editorial content and design to The Feminist Press; McGraw-Hill is responsible for distribution of the series to the high school audience, while The Feminist Press is responsible for distribution to colleges, bookstores, libraries, and the general public.

In the summer of 1975, the final proposal—to produce for co-publication a series of twelve supplementary books and their accompanying teaching guides—was funded by the Ford Foundation and the Carnegie Corporation. Project officers Terry Saario and Viven Stewart were supportive and helpful throughout the life of the project. In 1978, The Feminist Press received funds from the National Endowment for the Humanities to help complete the project. Additional funds also were received from the Edward W. Hazen Foundation and from the Rockefeller Family Fund.

Once initial funding was obtained, The Feminist Press began its search for additional staff to work on the project. The small nucleus of existing staff working on the project was expanded as The Feminist Press hired new employees. The *Women's Lives / Women's Work* project staff ultimately included six people who remained for the duration of the project: Sue Davidson, Merle Froschl, Florence Howe, Elizabeth Phillips, Susan Trowbridge, and Alexandra Weinbaum. Mary Mulrooney, a member of the project staff through 1979, thereafter continued her work as a free-lance production associate for the duration of the project. We also wish to acknowledge the contributions of Dora Janeway Odarenko and Michele Russell, who were on staff through 1977; and Shirley Frank, a Feminist Press staff member who was a member of the project staff through 1979. Helen Schrader, also a Feminist Press staff member, participated on the project during its first year and kept financial records and wrote financial reports throughout the duration of the project.

The *Women's Lives / Women's Work* project staff adopted the methods of work and the decision-making structure developed by The Feminist Press staff as a whole. As a Press "work committee," the project met weekly to make decisions, review progress, discuss problems. The project staff refined the editorial direction of the project, conceptualized and devised guidelines for the books and teaching guides, and identified prospective authors. When proposals came in, the project staff read and evaluated the submissions and made decisions regarding them. Similarly, when manuscripts arrived, the project staff read and commented on them. Project staff members took turns drafting memoranda, reports, and other documents. And the design of the series grew out of the discussions and the ideas generated at the project meetings. The books, teaching guides, and other informational materials had the advantage, at significant stages of development, of the committee's collective direction.

Throughout the life of the project, The Feminist Press continued to function and grow. Individuals on staff who were not part of the *Women's Lives / Women's Work* project provided support and advice to the project: Jeanne Bracken, Brenda Carter, Ranice Crosby, Shirley Frank, Brett Harvey, Frances Kelley, Carol Levin, Kam Murrin, Karen Raphael, Marilyn Rosenthal, Helen Schrader, Nancy Shea, Nivia Shearer, Anita Steinberg, Sharon Wigutoff, and Sophie Zimmerman.

The process of evaluation by teachers and students before final publication was as important as the process for developing ideas into books. To this end, we produced testing editions of the books. Field-testing networks were set up throughout the United States in a variety of schools—public, private, inner-city, small town, suburban, and rural—to reach as diverse a student population as possible. We field tested in the following cities, regions, and states: Boston, Massachusetts; Tampa, Florida; Greensboro, North Carolina; Tucson, Arizona; Los Angeles, California; Eugene, Oregon; Seattle, Washington; Shawnee Mission, Kansas; Martha's Vineyard, Massachusetts; New York City; Long Island; New Jersey; Rhode Island; Michigan; Minnesota. We also had an extensive network of educators—350 teachers across the country—who reviewed the books in the series, often using sections of books in classrooms. From teachers' comments, from students' questionnaires, and from tapes of teachers' discussions, we gained valuable information both for revising the books and for developing the teaching guides.

Although there is no easy way to acknowledge the devotion and enthusiasm of hundreds of teachers who willingly volunteered their time and energies, we would like to thank the following teachers—and their students—with whom we worked directly in the testing of *Household and Kin: Families in Flux.* In Kansas, David Wolfe, District Social Studies Supervisor, helped to contact the following teachers in the Shawnee Mission school district: Vicki Arndt-Helgesen, Jerry Hollembeak, Warren Knutson, Mike Ruggles, John Seevers, Pat Spillman, Marjorie Webb. In Michigan, Jo Jacobs, Coordinator, Office for Sex Equity in Education—with the assistance of Karla Atkinson and Karen Cottledge—helped to contact the following teachers in schools throughout the state: Jo Ann Burns, Mary Ellen Clery, Frances Deckard, Suzanne du Bois, Karen Fenske, Del Gerhardt, Pat Geyer, Shirley Harkless, Sylvia Lawhorn, Susan McFarland, Lenore Morkam, Bert

Montiegel, Florence Pangborn, Rose Riopelle, Judy Rogers, Ruth Valdes, Joan· Von Holten. In Minnesota, Don Hadfield, Specialist, Equal Educational Opportunities Section, State Department of Education, helped to contact the following teachers: Sonja Anderson, Edward Bauman, Barbara Braham, Colleen Clymer, Katharine Dumas, Judie Hanson, Sandy Johnson, Maya Jones, Gary Olsen, Kathryn Palmer, Dorothy Rock.

Three times during the life of the *Women's Lives / Women's Work* project, an Advisory Board composed of feminist educators and scholars met for a full day to discuss the books and teaching guides. The valuable criticisms and suggestions of the following people who participated in these meetings were essential to the project: Mildred Alpern, Rosalynn Baxandall, Peggy Brick, Ellen Cantarow, Elizabeth Ewen, Barbara Gates, Clarisse Gillcrist, Elaine Hedges, Nancy Hoffman, Susan Klaw, Alice Kessler-Harris, Roberta Kronberger, Merle Levine, Eleanor Newirth, Judith Oksner, Naomi Rosenthal, Judith Schwartz, Judy Scott, Carroll Smith-Rosenberg, Adria Steinberg, Barbara Sussman, Amy Swerdlow. We also want to express our gratitude to Shirley McCune and Nida Thomas, who acted -in a general advisory capacity and made many useful suggestions; and to Kathryn Girard and Kathy Salisbury who helped to develop the teacher and student field-testing questionnaires.

One person in particular whom we wish to thank for her work on *Household and Kin* is Flavia Rando for her exhaustive photo research and her unbounded enthusiasm for the job. Indeed, her research unearthed so many excellent photographs that it was with great difficulty that we limited ourselves to the ones that we finally selected for this volume.

Others whom we want to acknowledge are Ariane R. Berman for the cover illustration; Ruth Adam for restoration of the historical photographs; Charles Carmony, who prepared the index; Miriam Hurewitz, who copyedited the manuscript; Angela Kardovich and Randi Book of McGraw-Hill for administrative assistance; and Miriam Weintraub and Les Glass of Weinglas Typography Company for the text composition.

The work of the many people mentioned in these acknowledgments has been invaluable to us. We would also like to thank all of you who read this book—because you helped to create the demand that made the *Women's Lives / Women's Work* project possible.

THE FEMINIST PRESS

Authors' Acknowledgments

THE WRITING OF THIS BOOK was both an individual and a collaborative labor, so our acknowledgments are both personal and collective. First, we acknowledge our ongoing four-way dialogue for the critical affirmation we gave and received from one another. Working together not only sharpened our questions and broadened our inquiry, but it also made our individual research and writing a social process, more pleasurable and enriching than we had anticipated. There are also many people outside our small collective who helped us. We wish to thank the women's movement for asking again and again, "Who are we to one another? How can we live together in ways that are not oppressive?" These questions certainly shaped our consciousness, as it shapes family life today. Our collective thanks go to our editor, Elizabeth Phillips, for her active interest in our method and our work, and for her insights, support, and patience. Florence Howe made the original suggestion that initiated this analysis of families in flux, and we owe much to her vision and encouragement.

Joan Kelly acknowledges Martin Fleisher, Eve Fleisher, Blanche Cook, Clare Coss, Ruth Meyers, Rayna Rapp, and Stanley Swerdlow for their careful reading of her manuscript and for their fruitful suggestions.

Renate Bridenthal thanks the following people for giving generously of their time to read and discuss earlier drafts of her essay: Jacqueline Bernard, Constance Blake, Penny Cinancaneli, Blanche Cook, James Creane, JoAnne Magdoff, Kelsey Blumenstock Nieves, Myra Page, Nancy Romer, Annette Rubinstein, and Frederica Wachsberger. Special thanks are due to Patricia, Joe, and Joseph Quercia, whose spirited family discussion provided important feedback at an early stage, and to Hoby Spalding, her "family of choice."

Amy Swerdlow acknowledges and thanks Stanley, Joan, Ezra, Lisa, and Tom Swerdlow for the important things they taught her about family life that cannot be found in books. Amy Swerdlow and Phyllis Vine are both indebted to Alice Kessler-Harris, Ruth Meyers, and Florence Howe for their reading of the manuscript and their suggestions and comments. Special thanks go to the Lesbian Herstory Archives for making their collection available.

Introduction

Is THE AMERICAN FAMILY an endangered species, or is it a healthy organism adapting new forms to meet changing social conditions? Everyone, from high school teachers to senior citizens, from scholars to TV commentators, from social policy planners to school psychologists, is worrying about the American family and its ability to survive.

But what is the family? Is it, as some elementary school reading books have suggested, Dick and Jane at school, mommy in the kitchen baking cookies, and daddy at the factory or office "earning the dough"? Or is the family that larger network of grandparents, uncles, aunts, and cousins who may live in different households, but who come together for holidays, weddings, and funerals, and who offer each other support and solace in times of crisis?

Who defines what a family is? Is it the government, popular opinion, or one's own set of religious and moral beliefs that helps one to decide whether two people who are not biologically or legally related, but who share a home, financial resources, and commitment over time, are a family, an unmarried couple, or roommates?

"The family" seems to have many overlapping levels of meaning, just as it has a variety of forms and a multiplicity of functions. People's perceptions of the family usually reflect their racial, ethnic, and class backgrounds, their personal experiences of family and home. Most people know through their own experience and observation that family, on one level, does not necessarily mean people who live under the same roof or share resources. Relatives or kin are family. When older siblings leave home to set up their own households, they remain part of the family, as do mothers or fathers who leave because of divorce. Uncles, aunts, and cousins, even if they are seen rarely, are counted as part of the family network. On another level, however, most people understand family as related, in some way, to household. If we turn to the U.S. Bureau of the Census for help in defining the family, we find that the government considers family to be a group of two or more persons residing together who are related by blood, marriage, or adoption. On the other hand, if we look into the *Oxford English Dictionary*, we find that the English word "family" comes from the Latin *familia*, meaning household, and *famulus*, meaning servant. In fact, for centuries the English used the word "family" to mean not only the members of a household who were related by blood or by law, but servants as well. An old European peasant saying defines the family in a similar way as "those who eat from the same pot." A more recent definition cited by Renate Bridenthal in chapter two of this volume, "The Family Tree," comes from the *Journal of Home Economics*. It describes the family as a unit of intimate, transacting, and interdependent persons, sharing resources, responsibility, and commitment over time. This view has the virtue of including the growing number of unmarried couples of any sexual preference now living together, as well as those who live in communes and cooperative households. It is, for the purpose of this volume, perhaps the most useful definition of family. To put it more succinctly then, family is a *household of interdependent persons, sharing responsibilities and commitment to each other over time.*

The concept of family is so much a part of one's psychological and cultural inheritance that the very word evokes intense emotions. Feelings of love and pain, memories of good times and bad, a sense of loyalty and obligation tend to blur one's vision. It is difficult, even for those trained in social analysis, to view the family unemotionally and to examine it merely as a social institution.

The idea of the family is also overlaid with centuries of religious and moral belief handed down by parents, teachers, and religious leaders. To those who come out of the Judaic-Christian traditions, a look back at the patriarchs of the Old Testament or the Holy Family of the New Testament gives the impression that the patriarchal family in its nuclear form (father, mother, child) or in its extended form (grandparents, father, mother, children, aunts, uncles, cousins) has been the primary unit of social organization since the beginning of time.

Yet, today, many people find themselves living in families or households far different from those described in the Bible or in the more recent "Dick and Jane" readers. According to a report by the U.S. Bureau of the Census, in 1978, eleven million children were living in households headed only by a mother, while one million were living with their fathers alone. Population experts are predicting that nearly half of all children born today will, before the age of eighteen, spend a significant portion of their lives living with only one parent. As divorced mothers and fathers remarry and reorganize their households, millions will also be living in new households with one biological parent and one "step" parent. And, if present trends continue, a growing number of today's children will, when they become adults, postpone marriage and live, for a while, either in single-person households or as unmarried couples.

Important changes are also taking place in family roles. Many more mothers are in the paid labor force today than ever before. This means that they are helping to support their families financially and spending less time doing domestic chores and caring for children. The 1978 Census Bureau report revealed that mothers with preschool children are the fastest growing category of workers entering the paid labor force.

Thus we can see, through personal observations and through statistical surveys, that family organization, household membership, and sex roles are changing. But the tasks the family is expected to perform remain the same. In our society the family is still the primary institution responsible for nurturing and socializing babies and young children. It provides shelter for all its members, as well as necessary care, physical replenishment, and emotional support for those adults who go forth each day to work outside the home. Those who work outside the household not only provide the community's goods and services, but also bring back to the family the funds that enable the family to buy goods and services that insure survival. So the family is also the primary unit of consumption in our society.

Despite the proliferation of hospitals and social welfare agencies, the family remains the major resource for the care of the sick, the handicapped, and the aged. For better or for worse, in sickness or in health, the family is still, for most people, a refuge and a support system when the outside world becomes too much to handle. The family home is, as the poet Robert Frost put it, "The place where, when you have to go there, they have to take you in."

It is not surprising, therefore, that the rapid changes in family forms which are not accompanied by changes in family functions are causing alarm. People are asking themselves, "Who will take care of the children in single-parent households or in families where both parents work outside the home?" "Who will care for us and love us as we grow old, if we choose not to marry or raise children?" "Where can we turn if our brothers, sisters, fathers, and mothers are scattered in different places?" "Are there ways in which families can be organized that will be more suitable to our changing needs?" "What will be the options for love and security when today's children become the parent generation?"

One can begin to answer these questions only when one examines the ways in which the family interacts with the economy, the state, and the culture. Today, with society in flux, and with the economy, the government, cultural institutions, and the family often in contradiction with each other, it is a particularly appropriate time to take a new, hard look at the family, to analyse its forms and functions in relation to each other, to examine its past and present—and to separate the myths from the reality.

This book attempts to take such a searching and analytical look at the family in flux. The authors have tried to peel away layers of ideology and emotion in order to uncover the bare bones, those basic combinations of sexual, psychological, personal, historical, social, and economic relations we call "the family." Using the tools of social historians, the authors have looked at the lives of people in the past to see the variety of familial structures human beings have devised. These different structures are analysed in relation to the society's economic and social organization.

Looking back to the past to trace the historical development of family forms and family ideology, reviewing and analysing the variety of family relationships in the United States today, and examining utopian alternatives to the so-called traditional family, all three chapters of this book reveal that there is no such thing as a normative or universal family. The family is a human invention, a social creation, a set of relationships that changes over time with economic, political, and social developments.

Joan Kelly's historical and anthropological investigation reveals that the ways in which a particular society organizes its familial relations, including reproduction and consumption, depend, to a large extent, on the ways in which that society organizes its production. In other words, how a given people earn their living—whether they till the soil or work in offices and factories, whether they are feudal serfs or wage laborers, whether they produce together as household units or send some members out of the house to earn wages—affects the size of the household, the division of labor by sex and age, and patterns of child rearing. The way in which property in a particular society is divided or transmitted also affects power relations within the family, gender roles, and attitudes toward sexual behavior, particularly of women and children.

Renate Bridenthal's analysis of the family today shows how class, race, and culture play a central role in determining a family's structure and ideology. A family's place in the socio-economic order influences its size, attitudes toward sexuality, if the mother works outside the home, how children are raised and educated, how resources are shared, and how the nuclear unit relates to its extended kin. Bridenthal's research reveals that the so-called traditional nuclear unit is today most characteristic of middle-class families. The poor and the rich tend to interact with extended kin networks, each for different reasons.

In chapter three of this volume, Amy Swerdlow and Phyllis Vine explore the centuries-old search for an ideal family form. They have found, in examining literary utopias, intentional communitarian societies, and contemporary communes, that proposals for family reform, even the most utopian and vision-ary, are tied to the political and economic needs and the ideology and consciousness of their time. There is, however, one theme that underlies a large number of alternative proposals, from the days of Plato to the 1970s. That is the conviction that most traditional family forms both mirror and recreate authoritarian relations, economic and social competition, and the oppression of women. Therefore, those seeking more equality in the economy or in the state have often turned to experiments with alternative sexual practices, child-rearing arrangements, and household organization. These familial experiments have never been widespread, but their existence, both in literature and life, serves to remind us again that the family is a malleable institution.

As we perceive that the family is not only a product of the larger society, but also its producer and reproducer, we begin to realize that changing the family can help change the society. As Joan Kelly concludes in chapter one, "Every generation has to find its own way of shaping its institutions." Knowledge of the great variety of family forms human beings have devised in the past, the many different kinds of families that exist today, and the utopian visions of the past, present, and future can give us a larger sense of the possibilities and the choices before us.

AMY SWERDLOW

Household
and Kin

Families in Flux

ONE: Family Life

A Historical Perspective

By Joan Kelly

FOR MOST OF US, the family meets many of our needs for love and support. We tend to think that all families do this in the same way. Yet families are almost as varied as people. Families differ from society to society, and they have changed over time. The anthropologist Claude Lévi-Strauss demonstrated this in a famous essay called *The Family*.[1] He noted that anthropologists once thought that "the family, consisting of a more or less durable union, socially approved, of a man, a woman, and their children, is a universal phenomenon, present in each type of society." But, he pointed out, this definition excludes many people. In the case of the Nayar, for example, a people from the Malabar coast of India, marriages were only symbolic. The warrior life of the men kept them away from home. Their wives were expected to take lovers, and children belonged exclusively to their mother's kin group or matrilineage.

The family arrangements of ancient Sparta were similar to those of the Nayar. The military organization of Spartan society required adult men to live most of their lives in barracks. Their wives lived in households with children whose paternity no one was too strict about, and same-sex love relationships were highly valued. Obviously, the definition of family that the anthropologists started with was too narrow. It was, in fact, a definition of today's nuclear family—which is not universal at all. If we look at the family historically, and in different societies today, we reach the same conclusion Lévi-Strauss did. The only universal element he could find about families was that human beings always form them.

Here we will look at some of the kinds of families people have established. We will see how people form relations of love and caring, how they have and rear children in families, and how they carry out their society's forms of work by way of families. The patterns of family relations that emerge—of who is considered kin, who lives with and cares for whom, and what is the basic unit for producing and consuming—turn out to be wonderfully varied and frequently changing, even at this very moment.

Kinds of Families

The great variety of family patterns and some of the reasons for it stand out very clearly when we look at societies studied by anthropologists and historians. We will, therefore, first examine families in tribal societies. Then we will turn to family forms that preceded our own, in medieval and modern Europe and the United States. We will see how today's nuclear family emerged out of feudal and preindustrial times. In this historical perspective, we may better understand how the nuclear family developed as it did, why it is undergoing such profound changes, and how the family as we know it might continue to evolve.

Kinship in Tribal Societies. Many tribal societies still exist in parts of Africa, Asia, Oceania, and among the native peoples of the Americas. The question of kin, or who one's relatives are, is more important in tribal society than any other matter. Tribal societies are organized by kin, and life is shaped by the family to which one belongs. Indeed, the question of kin is so elaborate and varied, that it allows one to see how even the relation between children and parents is socially, rather than biologically, formed.

Paternal authority over children as we define it is the authority of a biological father over his children. This form of authority is nonexistent in many places. Among the Nayar, for example, it is the mother's brother who is economically responsible for, and has authority over, his sister's children. The biological father has only a ritual relation to his offspring.

This denial of paternal power goes so far among the Trobriand Islanders and the Wunambal of northwestern Australia, that it is an official belief of both societies that men play no role in the biological conception of children. Such beliefs need not be due to ignorance. They are probably another way of asserting that the maternal uncle is the only socially recognized male parent.

Children in certain parts of Tibet and Nepal have a different kind of male parent. Men are seminomadic here. They work as guides and bearers of goods and are off in the mountains for long parts of the year. Several men, usually brothers, marry the same woman, who keeps a common household for them. This marital arrangement of one woman with several husbands is called polyandry. All the children regard as "father" the husband who officially becomes father of the household by a special family ceremony. In this case, we speak of a social father. Fatherhood is recognized, but it is not a biological matter. It is socially agreed upon, and the position may be transferred to another of the husbands by means of the same ceremony.

Another example of how the relation of father is socially rather than biologically formed is in a family where children have one woman as mother and another woman as father. Among several peoples of Africa, such as the Fou of Dahomey and the Lovedu of South Africa, women of high rank marry "wives" who bear children to them by unacknowledged lovers.[2] The noble woman is regarded as the "father" of the children. In accordance with the father's right in those societies, she passes on to "her" children, whom the wives bear, her name, status, and wealth.

In none of these cases does biological paternity lead to fatherhood in the sense of special emotional ties, economic responsibility, and authority over children. The biological father is not a parent to his children in ways that we would recognize.

Motherhood tends to be a more stable matter. The biological mother is usually the socially recognized mother, too. However, females other than the mother often take on maternal responsibilities. Child rearing tends to be a community activity in the more egalitarian, tight knit communities of tribal society. Even nursing is shared. Children nursed by several women often regard these women as their "other mothers." These may be their mother's sisters, as in south and central Australia. Or, in polygamous societies such as the Tupi-Kawahib of central

Brazil, the several wives of a chief act as mother to all the children.

Collective mothering also occurs in societies where children are raised in matrilineal houses. This arrangement is common among horticultural people who live by cultivating plants and raising some animals for food. The longhouses of the Iroquois of North America held twenty-five or so mother/children units, in villages of about 2,000 people. The houses and the children raised in them belonged to the mother's line of descent. A husband moved into the house of his wife—and moved out again if the conjugal unit of wife and husband dissolved, which it frequently did. Among the Iroquois, the matrilineal household was a far stronger family unit than that of mother, father, and children.[3]

The Atjehnese of Sumatra have a similar pattern of matrilineal kin and households.[4] In place of longhouses, they live in separate huts that cluster in compounds. The huts and compounds belong to sisters and mothers' sisters. Ownership of the houses and often of the rice land the women cultivate passes through the maternal line to daughters. The Atjehnese women control the group's basic means of subsistence, much as the Iroquois matrons were in charge of the distribution of food and other stores. Hence, women in both cases enjoy the authority that goes with economic power.

In societies organized by kinship, then, as most tribal societies are, children's relation to their father and mother may vary. They may be subject mainly to maternal authority; to matrilineal authority exercised by the mother's brother, as well as by the mother and her sisters; or to paternal authority exercised by a ritually chosen father—who may at times be a woman. The children's household may be a collective one in which the girls may remain but the boy will have to leave. Or, in yet another variation, children may be reared in an individual household by their biological mother and father, both of whom are socially recognized as their parents.

Growing Up in Feudal Society. Feudal societies existed in early Greece from the fifteenth to the twelfth century B.C., in

Japan from the twelfth to the sixteenth century A.D., and in medieval Europe from the late fifth to the fourteenth century.[5] Although economic and political life was organized by alliances among kin groups, in feudal society a small minority of such groups, who possessed military power, controlled almost all the landed property and wealth. This warrior aristocracy exercised sovereign power—of war and peace, life and death, and taxation— over the populations that worked the land for them. This contrasts with the more communal tribal societies where there were (and are) no great distinctions in wealth and power. In political terms, feudalism is thus seen as intermediate between tribal, kinship society and class-based society organized by a state (called a *polis* by the Greeks, giving us our word *political*). In its family patterns, too, feudal society was both distinctive and intermediate. Its organization by kin groups gave certain families and the women in them powers they would lose as states developed. The sharp class divisions of feudal society, however, kept military and economic power in the hands of a very few families.

In the case of medieval Europe, family life differed greatly depending on whether one belonged to the warrior aristocracy or the laboring serf class. It also took different forms for those who entered the Church. These three social groups were called "the estates" in feudal Europe. The clergy was the first estate. The warrior aristocracy was the second, and the laboring class, mostly serfs, made up the third estate. Children were reared very differently to fit them for these very different stations in life.

Children of the ruling aristocracy were trained to advance the powers and class positions of their kin, or family line—chiefly by arms, but also by marriage and by means of high position in the Church. The aristocracy ruled over its counties, duchies, towns, and territories by a complicated system of exchange. Great lords (or, sometimes, ladies) gave lands "in fief" to vassals. The vassal, who was always a warrior, or male member of the aristocracy, governed the fief, which might consist of one or many units of manorial land. Income from the fief supported the vassal and his warrior dependents, but the vassal never owned the lands he held from his lord. Vassals had to give military service and other

dues in return for a fief, and this bond between vassal and lord
could always be renewed, or broken.

Sometimes, vassalage coincided with kin ties, but often it did
not. The warrior class was itself divided into ranks that ranged
from mere knights to powerful counts, dukes, barons, and
members of royal families. Within the aristocracy, individuals
advanced themselves and their family line by allying with more
powerful, higher-ranking families. Vassalage and marriage were
two ways these kin groups made political alliances with each
other.

To serve the needs of their family line, children of the
aristocracy were sent away from their parental households when
they were very young. At about eight or ten years of age, but
sometimes even earlier, they joined a household of superior
rank. This might be the "court" or residence of their father's lord,
of a powerful maternal uncle, or of a ducal or a royal family.
Education at court consisted in part of training in arms, for
warfare. The tournaments and jousting of the Middle Ages were
displays of this kind of skill. Girls often became skilled at
weapons and riding, too, because they could, and often did, take
over fiefs to preserve the family property in the absence of male
heirs, or when their husbands went off to war. Because noble-
women could serve their kin and husbands as managers and/or
heirs of fiefs, they had genuine power in medieval society—
particularly in the higher ranks of the aristocracy. This gave
them a commanding position in the second major area of courtly
education: training in courtesy, or chivalry. Children, and all
those residing at court, were expected to develop manners
befitting their noble way of life, and it was largely ladies at court
who shaped these courteous manners.

Courtesy included courtly love, which has had a great
influence on modern notions of romance. In medieval society,
however, this love relationship was not connected with marriage. Young knights were encouraged to devote themselves to
the love of a lady at court, who might often be the lady of their
lord. This is the case in the most famous romances of the time,
such as that of Lancelot and Guinevere or of Tristan and Isolde.[6]
In these stories, adultery is clearly idealized as a form of love. Yet

courtly love actually supported the institutions of the feudal warrior aristocracy. From his service to his lady, the lover was supposed to learn how to be faithful and self-sacrificing—the primary virtues of any vassal. Moreover, men were away a great deal of the time in this warrior society, and marriages were political alliances, not emotional ones. The courtly romances probably reflect an acceptance of extramarital love that responded to these situations and to the fact that children were assets in feudal society, as potential warriors and wives. If children should be born out of wedlock, they were usually adopted formally or informally as members of their biological father's family line, or they were accepted in their mother's household as children of her and her husband's line.

The development of courtly love was opposed by the Church in medieval and early modern Europe, although not too successfully.[7] Because the Church held that its nuns and monks, and all members of the clergy, should be celibate or nonsexual, it did not reproduce itself biologically. Its ranks had to be filled from the aristocracy and peasantry. The Church claimed that celibacy was a spiritually superior state. This seemed to entitle its members to superior social status. Indeed, the Church, which was one of the greatest landowners of medieval Europe, sought to rule over the kings and emperors of the feudal aristocracy, as well as over serfs. The religious life officially excluded sexuality. This kept the Church's wealth from falling into the hands of heirs. The sexual views of the Church also kept women out of the clergy. Although women could be nuns and could rule over convents and convent lands as abbesses, women could not be priests, bishops, or popes.

The Church sought to limit sex for the laity to heterosexual union, and to make that union a lifelong, monogamous marriage. It permitted sexuality only for procreation. In this sense, the Church tended to strengthen family ties among wife, husband, and children. It opposed extramarital love, as well as the aristocracy's frequent use of divorce to gain new lands and allies by way of new marriages. At the same time, for children moving into adulthood, the Church offered an alternative to marriage and family. The Church or convent became a substitute family for those who entered it. Noble families sent daughters and younger sons who would not inherit land into the Church, where they assumed powerful positions as bishops, abbots, and abbesses. Those children of serfs who served the Church moved into more lowly positions. They became priests on manors, or humble nuns and monks.

Like children sent away to court, many children destined for the Church began their training quite young. In convents and cathedral schools, upper-class children, and some from the lower ranks, learned Latin—which was the language of the Church, and also the only written prose language until the thirteenth century. When universities developed in the course of the twelfth century, they were open only to those who had this basic Latin training. University students were educated for high positions in the church hierarchy, and for positions within the universities themselves. They were all clerics or clergy. As clerics, university students were all men. Education in civil law was the only area of learning open from the first to lay people. Even though in later centuries, higher education was opened to lay people, certain clerical attitudes have clung to academic life. With very few exceptions, women were excluded from higher education down to the late nineteenth century, and only in the twentieth century have fellowships come to be held by students who are not unmarried men. Even today, medieval caps and gowns are worn at graduations.

Neither training at court, nor at church schools, was open to the large majority of young people in feudal society, male or female. While the Church prayed for the "soul" of feudal Christian society, and the aristocracy "protected" or controlled it by force of its arms, the third estate or social group, mostly serfs and some few artisans and merchants, fed that society. The labor of the third estate supported the Church and the aristocracy. The serfs tilled the lands of medieval Europe, and for their children there was no education except in the tasks that enabled them to replace their parents.

The status of the serfs was midway between slavery and personal freedom. They were bound, not to individual owners, but to the manors on which they were born. Every serf family had its own cottage and its own lands to till. But, in addition, serfs paid a variety of rents and taxes in the form of labor, as well as in animals and food. They had to pay a tithe, or tenth part of their income, to the Church and do heavy labor for the manor besides. They worked the lord's land as well as their own. They kept the walls of the lord's castle in repair, built the roads, and carted wine and supplies to their lord's lord. They paid their lord each time they used the manor's mill to grind their grain. They paid for the oven to bake their bread, the press to make their wine. And it was the lord's manorial court that tried and fined—or executed—them.

Because for centuries there was more land than there were peasants to cultivate it, marriage outside the manor was forbidden. This ensured that children would take over the labor of their parents. Thus, serf children were raised in their family cottage and worked alongside their parents from early childhood. Their life was confined to the manor, its village, and the local church. And with life defined by the daily and seasonal round of work on the land, they had little time for play or self-cultivation, except for Sundays and holy days.[8]

The Preindustrial Household. In Europe in the fifteenth and sixteenth centuries, feudalism was replaced by state-organized societies, although vestiges of the feudal system remained for centuries. With this shift came changes in the nature of the family. The household with its resources—usually land—became the basic unit of economic production. In place of the common lands of a tribal village, or the medieval manor which supported several serf families as well as its lord, private property emerged. That is, the individual household-family owned its own means of subsistence.[9]

In this preindustrial household, the position of men, and especially of the father, was greatly strengthened. The father owned the household and its resources. Usually he passed it on to his sons—either to the eldest, by primogeniture, or to as many as he wished. During this period, laws were enacted that favored inheritance in the male line. State laws also supported paternal authority in the household. Hence sex, as well as kin and class, shaped in new ways the experience of family members.

Because of the power vested in the father in the preindustrial household, this type of family is called patriarchal (from *pater*, the Roman word for father). The patriarchal family contrasts with the matrilineage of the Iroquois and Atjehnese, for example, and with the family organization of medieval Europe too. Although feudal society recognized paternal authority, an aristocratic wife's kin protected her interests, and everyone treated children more as members of the family line than as property of their fathers. Women and children of medieval serf families belonged as much to their lord (who might be a lady) as to their husbands and fathers. Widows and daughters in both classes could inherit the positions of men as long as they carried out the services that went with them. And in both serf and aristocratic families, fathers did not own their family property (which really belonged to the manor or to their lord), so they could not dispose of it at will.

As state-organized societies developed, the privately owned property that most often sustained the work of the patriarchal household was land. Some households also supported themselves through craft production. Many farming families in England, for example, worked the land but also spun and wove cloth at home which they sold to merchants. Merchants, artisans, and shopkeepers in the sixteenth, seventeenth, and eighteenth centuries combined home and workplace in a similar way, although their property was not in land. This small group was called the bourgeoisie in Europe, from the towns or *bourgs* (Cherbourg, Edinburgh, Strassbourg) in which their way of life developed. Or they were called "middle class," because they were midway between the serfs who were not free and the aristocracy who were free but did not labor. They were free, but they had to work for a living. Typically, these members of the bourgeoisie worked with property that their families owned. Their households usually consisted of a shop or store, with living space in the rear or on the upper floor. The father generally owned the household and passed it on to one or more of his sons. Most of the members of the family, along with apprentices, lived in the household and worked at the craft or business together.

The poor of sixteenth-, seventeenth-, and eighteenth-century Europe and America also supported themselves within the patriarchal household. Since the poor had little or no property of their own, they worked and often lived in someone else's household. They were often bound to their work, or indentured, but unlike medieval serfs and American slaves, their period of service was limited. Poor children left their parents at an early age to begin their service in another's household. From seven years on, they labored for masters who provided work, room, and board—and discipline as well. They worked as farmhands, apprentices, and, if they were girls, as domestic servants. Apprentices in the crafts were usually indentured at fourteen for a period of seven years. At the end of their period of service, these young people hoped to have training in some skill or craft, or to have acquired some land and small items of furnishings with which to form a household of their own.

Heads of households—usually fathers of its core nuclear family—had the same authority over indentured youths and live-in laborers as they had over their own children and relatives. Everyone who dwelt and worked within a household obeyed the father as if he were parent to them all. In 1715, Daniel Defoe described that paternal power this way: "Masters of families are parents, that is guardians and governors, to their whole house, though they are fathers only to their children."[10] Hence, fathers were often called "the Governor." English farm wives referred to their husbands as "Master" well into the nineteenth century,[11] and even older parents or single brothers supported by a father's household bowed to his authority.

As masters, fathers could be tyrants, and many were brutal. Whipping, flogging, and child beating were common in the preindustrial patriarchal household. The propertied classes of the time believed in "breaking the will" even of their own children. It is from them we learn that "to spare the rod spoils the child," and they certainly did not spare the foster children and live-in servants who worked for them.

Not all people could be, or wanted to be, supported and governed in this paternal way. But state laws and need for work pressured them to do so. In seventeenth-century New England, where the settlers could easily regulate their small populations, it is claimed that virtually everyone who was not a household head or his kin was the servant or apprentice of one. It is in New England, too, that the relation of household work to marriage and sexual activity is clearest. Apprentices, lodgers, and domestic servants were expected—like children—to live with their masters until they had acquired the means to marry and form households of their own. Until that time, the master was supposed to guard their chastity, for Puritan New England in particular frowned upon sexual activity outside of marriage.[12]

Paternal control of sexuality is common wherever we find the patriarchal household/family. The father controls the marriages and sexual lives, as well as the work lives, of all members of the household in ways that best support its economy. It is to his interest, and the interest of the household economy, that young men marry late. Sons under this system often delay marriage until their late twenties or thirties, until the father parcels out some of his land to them, or passes the homestead on. Live-in laborers must wait until they have earned enough to buy land or other means of subsistence to start their own households. In the meantime, the young men give the patriarch the labor he needs.

Girls and women are just as strictly controlled in this kind of family. They have no hope of heading a household, as long as the pattern of inheritance favors their brothers and sons, as it did in Europe and the United States. In the sixteenth, seventeenth, and eighteenth centuries, propertied families therefore sent their daughters to households more prosperous than their own, to do some kind of service. They might be companions—really personal maids—to the woman of the household. Or they might be governesses. Poorer girls were placed quite young in other people's households to do spinning or domestic work.

Young women often found their future husbands among associates in the households they went to. Their marriages were arranged either by their own father or by the master. Girls or women who did not find husbands could look forward only to continued domestic or other work, in their parental or other households. Marriage seemed preferable, because it put a woman in charge of the domestic arrangements of her husband's household. She might be called the mistress of the household, although it was "his" household, and wives were expected to give obedient service. Peasant wives all over Europe did not sit at the table when the husband and boys ate; they served them.

In all these situations, the sexual life of girls and women was supervised by heads of households who were usually male. This sometimes led to abuse, particularly if the household was very powerful or isolated. Then the local community could not act as a restraint the way the small medieval village or town could. In other cases, paternal authority led to strict sexual suppression. Unlike the aristocratic feudal family, there was no room in the preindustrial household for children born outside of marriage. The preindustrial family's resources were more limited; and whatever the sum of household property, it had to be divided among "legitimate" male heirs.

For the vast majority of Europeans and Americans in the sixteenth, seventeenth, and eighteenth centuries, the household and its resources formed the pattern of work and family life. As the basic economic unit for most people, it tended to make the family synonymous with whoever lived and worked within the household, rather than with groups of kin.

The preindustrial household, however, did not form the pattern of family life either for the most privileged or for the most oppressed. The aristocratic families of Europe did not live unto themselves in a household, or support themselves by its means. Aristocrats often lived at royal and princely courts. They continued to send their children to court and convents for their early training, and moved their young men into high-ranking positions in the Church, the military, and the government. Until the French Revolution and even later, until they ceased to be a legal ruling class, the aristocracy considered their kin group or lineage to be their family. And they maintained the class status of their lineage by marrying only into other aristocratic families. Ever since the age of courtly love, their sexual practices had been quite free. This was due in part to their privileged position in society, but also to the fact that marriage for them served chiefly the class interests of the family line. It had little to do with household economy, or even with bonds of affection and sexuality. Indeed, marriage was often ruled out altogether for younger daughters and sons of the aristocracy so as to keep the landed estates of the family line intact.

At the other end of the social scale, the slaves of the southern United States had neither the property nor the personal freedom that formed the basis of the preindustrial household. They were themselves property of the landed proprietors they worked for. And they lived in shacks on the master's land, unlike indentured servants who lived in the household of a master for their limited term of service. The Afro-American slaves raised their children in two-parent families when they could, however.[13] Their domestic ties were close-knit, even though these ties were often cruelly severed by forcible sale. Teenage children were most likely to be sold out of the family, but marriages between young parents could also be broken. From letters that have been preserved, we get some sense of how frequent and painful these separations were. One family could not be reunited after emancipation, for example, because the husband had married again after he was sold to a new owner. "I would come and see you," he wrote to his first wife,

but I know you could not bear it. I want to see you and I don't want to see you. I love you just as well as I did the last day I saw you, and it will not do for you and I to meet. I am married, and my wife have two children, and if you and I meets it would make a very dissatisfied family.

Send me some of the children's hair in a separate paper with their names on the paper. Will you please git married as long as I am married. My dear, you know the Lord knows both of our hearts. You know it never was our wishes to be separated....[14]

Black slave families also formed strong kin networks. By naming children after fathers, aunts, grandparents, and other blood kin in both the maternal and paternal lines, they kept track of family members forcibly separated by sale. Kin networks also provided the comfort of family connections to slaves sold into another locality. The web of strong domestic and kin ties formed by Afro-Americans made possible their emotional and, later, their economic survival in a hostile surrounding community.

Class, or social status, may thus account for departures from what the rest of a society takes to be the family norm. In other instances, changes in the norm come about as a society at large begins to adjust to new social developments. Population changes, such as changes in sex ratio due to war or to a prohibition of infanticide, may affect traditional patterns of marriage and work. Polygamy tends to occur when there are more women than men, for example. And the polyandrous situation of one wife to several brothers that was common in parts of Tibet and Nepal grew up in a context of girl infanticide.

Changes in family form also come about with changes in patterns of work. These may be due to the loss or gain of property such as slaves, land, or mineral wealth, or to new ways of organizing work and property. When Europe and the United States industrialized, in the nineteenth and twentieth centuries, work and property were reorganized so drastically that we still call this process the industrial "revolution." It was then that the nuclear family developed—but not in the same way for all classes.

The Nuclear Family

Today's nuclear family descends from the preindustrial household/family. Industrialization was the main reason for the change in the family pattern of the household. With industrialization, goods and services came to be produced outside the household. The household ceased to be a center of production—although it remained as an economic and residential unit for its members.

First cloth and clothing, then all manner of goods, including the machinery for producing them, came to be made in factories rather than shops and homes. In factories, groups of workers were gathered in one place and organized to work together. Together, they produced large quantities of goods that had previously been produced by an individual or a small group of household workers. This is called social production, and it soon replaced privately organized household work.

The property that supported this new social production of goods changed, too. Instead of land and the handlooms and spinning machines of the farming household, instead of the simple tools and skills of the artisan, came the kind of property called capital. Industrial capital includes money, plant (factories and machinery), and raw materials. Large sums of money were needed to purchase machinery and raw materials like cotton, coal, and iron. Money paid for the labor that transformed raw materials into products that could be sold. And ever larger sums of money from the sale of those products were reinvested in new plants and more materials.

Separating Work and Home. England in the late eighteenth century, then western Europe and the United States, were the first to undergo this shift to social production. In increasing numbers, people went to work in factories and mines. They laid the railroads that formed a network for the exchange of materials and goods. And as they went to the new mill and mining towns and to the cities, they were forced to leave the land behind them. Farming and household production could no longer support them as it had for centuries. Society became urbanized with industrialization. In 1870, out of every 100 people ten years or older in the United States, there were 48 men and women who worked the land. In 1970, there were 3 farm workers out of every 100 people sixteen years or older in the United States.[15]

Agricultural products were still needed, of course. In fact, urban life stimulated farming and the raising of livestock, as city dwellers needed food. Large-scale agricultural businesses developed to meet the mass demand, particularly in the United States. That is, farming, too, became capitalized. By using expensive machinery, large agricultural businesses could produce more food than small household farms. They also required far fewer workers. Throughout the nineteenth and twentieth centuries, as farmers found they could not compete with the big agricultural businesses, they sold or abandoned their small family farms. This drove even more people to the cities to look for work.

Capital in the form of large sums of money, machinery, and materials thus came to provide the means of work for most people. The social organization of work, whether on the land or in factories, mines, and transportation industries, replaced much of the work once done in private households. And as cities developed, small family businesses—just like small family farms—gave way to larger, more powerful operations. Banks and stock companies, insurance and law firms, large department stores and food chains, financed, insured, and sold the new products of industrial society. Large numbers of white-collar workers were needed to sustain these growing businesses, and so in the early decades of the twentieth century, masses of people became clerks, stenographers, telephone operators, sales-persons, brokers, and lawyers. Their work, too, was socially organized.

In all forms of this socially organized work, people work outside the home. Wages are their means of support—in place of private family property in the form of land or small shops. Thus, the patriarchal preindustrial household lost its productive function. We are still experiencing the consequences of this major change in family life.

The most immediate consequence was that the household became merely a home. That is, it ceased to be a center of production, although it remained the center of family life. As the household lost its land or shop, most of its members also moved out by day (or night) to work for the wages that now bought their food and paid their rent. However, home was the place that supplied the sustenance, comforts, and necessities wage earners required to get to work the next day. Thus, some work remained in the home. The work of transforming the income and goods that came from outside into the necessities and pleasures of daily life—meals, clothing, decent living quarters—remained in the home. Such work was necessary to sustain the family and raise the next generation, and it was mostly women with children who stayed at home to do it.

The notion of who makes up a family changed, too. The family shrank in size as it gradually lost the apprentices, live-in laborers, and kin who had dwelt within the household when it was a place of employment. In preindustrial times, the members of a household were regarded as a family. As industrialization proceeded, only the nucleus of the patriarchal household/family remained at home. Gradually, the nuclear family of parents and children became the new family norm.

The Division of Family Labor. When work was separated from the home, the family ceased to work together as a unit. This divided the sexes and the generations from each other in new ways. Women and children worked in factories during the early stages of industrialization. After that, however, it was mostly men who had the jobs in factories, mines, and businesses. Woman's place was said to be in the home. Since children were also based in the home, they, too, were cut off from the work life of adult males. Socially organized production seemed to separate women from men, and children from their fathers, keeping women and children in the private domain of the home.

Historically, the exclusion of women and children from the world of social labor and public life occurred first in modern times in the wealthy bourgeois families of Europe. The feudal aristocracies knew no such division. Their court and manor houses were the centers of social and public life. Nor did most working people know any division between family and work. Labor was parceled out by sex and age in the serf family and in the later preindustrial household—but the workplace was not divided. This was as true of artisans and small shopkeepers as it was of peasants and farmers. Work and home were bound together, and so were the daily work lives of women and men, children and adults. But among the wealthy bourgeoisie in Europe, and by the nineteenth century in America, the divided pattern of the nuclear family emerged.

Originally, the owners of capital were called the upper middle class (or haute bourgeoisie in French). They were not considered the upper class as the aristocracy held that position. In the preindustrial period, this upper segment of the bourgeoisie invested in commerce, mining, and textile production, as well as in land. In the late eighteenth and nineteenth centuries, with industrialization, they put the wealth they had made in trade, banking, and other enterprises into the new factories, mines, and transportation systems. All these sites of capital investment were outside the home. The upper middle class defined this entire sphere of work as man's world. They extended this notion to the state, too. Politics was for them a male domain, just as it was a class domain from which workers and farmers were excluded.

This capitalist class became the dominant group, economically and politically, in nineteenth-century Europe and America. It became the real upper class, replacing the aristocracy of the past. As in the old aristocratic upper class, women in these capitalist families became "ladies," when their fathers, brothers, and husbands became wealthy and powerful. Doing no work outside the home, and with servants inside it, they were leisured like aristocratic women of the preindustrial period. Like them, they enjoyed a class privilege. But bourgeois women were more restricted than aristocratic women had been. They were considered domestic creatures at a time when men's activities were all outside the home. Their lives were more segregated from men's than aristocratic women's lives had been. The new ladies of the capitalist class and wives of the middling professional groups (lawyers, doctors, churchmen, and professors) who served them were told they had no role in the public world. Women's lives were confined to the private sphere and defined by the domestic functions of "consumption" and "reproduction."

The affluence of men was demonstrated by the cost of supporting women. By "conspicuous consumption," a newly arrived capitalist family gave notice to society that it was making its way into the ranks of the rich. The idleness of women, the servants they required to maintain them, their cumbersome dress and delicacy, were part of the display of bourgeois wealth and power. Even in the lower and middling middle classes, men gauged their status by whether or not they could affford to keep their wives and daughters at home. At home, bourgeois women were less idle than they seemed. They had a heavy burden of entertaining to aid their husbands' business and professional careers. Though hostessing—with its dinner parties, elaborate exchange of invitations and thank you's, and fine cuisine—falls under the category of consumption rather than production, for women it was work. It was work, too, to cater to the emotional needs of one's husband. And the most valued work of bourgeois women was in the sphere of reproduction—bearing and rearing children.

Indeed, motherhood was the *only* function society came to recognize for "ladies"—until women themselves forced a change.[16] The women's movement of the second half of the nineteenth and the early twentieth century was largely a struggle of upper-middle- and middle-class women to break out of the limits imposed by marriage and the mothering role. They demanded education and professional training, the right to work and be active outside the home, and control of their own income and property. At the same time, because the mothering role was so esteemed, many affluent women adopted it, but extended it to society at large. This was especially true in England and the United States. Florence Nightingale was one of many gifted women who worked tirelessly, often without pay or official position, to supply housing, schools, and health care to nineteenth-century children, workers, and soldiers. Women did volunteer work to meet the social needs that industrial capitalism created, but which business and political leaders ignored.

The energies of most upper-middle- and middle-class women in the nineteenth and early twentieth centuries were confined to the nuclear family, however.[17] Marriage was their means of support, and motherhood made them the vessel through which family ownership of property passed from generation to generation—in the male line. Bourgeois women did not inherit or control economically significant property. And in the late nineteenth century, they were just beginning to overcome educational barriers and laws that kept them out of business, the professions, and politics. Their rights of divorce were limited. They often had no claim to their children, and if they did separate from their husbands, they had little possibility of supporting themselves.

The economic dependency of women upon men could be a burden to bourgeois men, too. It bound men as well as women to marriage and made them solely responsible for the material well-being of their families. Yet marriage and family served men in many ways. Men had the economic rewards and public recognition of achievement in the world, as well as the comforts and rewards of home and family. A family—especially sons who would inherit their gains—gave them a reason for spending their lives on business. And at the end of days spent in hardheaded competition, they could return to the home as a refuge. Wives provided emotional support, tender sentiments, and a compliant relationship. A wife was supposed to be "the angel of the hearth," and children were to be seen but not heard.

Children also became economic dependents in the bourgeois home. Unlike children of working-class families, children of the rich, and even children of the growing middle class, did not have to go to work. Their leisure brought advantages and disadvantages. A childhood and adolescence without work made possible greater cultural development. On the other hand, it postponed adulthood. Economic dependency kept youths of the wealthier classes subject to the authority of their families, and that authority continued along patriarchal lines. Fathers kept their daughters at home well into the early twentieth century, while their sons went to boarding school and the university. But for both girls and boys, the bourgeois father was a forbidding, authoritative figure. He was distant, yet completely in command.

The distance of the bourgeois father was emotional as well as physical. Business outside the home kept him away from his children and absorbed his interests. Moreover, loving, supportive attitudes were supposed to be womanly, as well as unbusinesslike. At the same time, this often harsh, barely known person continued to control all the property of "his" family. This gave him a concern for, and power over, both the sexual lives and the careers of his children.

Girls were reared to marry a suitable member of the propertied class. Their social lives were closely watched and they were brought up in extreme modesty. The more "protected" and sexually ignorant they were, the more apt they would be to obey the will of their fathers. Even though the upper middle class widely accepted the double standard, according to which women had to adhere to a stricter moral code than men, fathers also controlled their sons' sexual lives. Daughters and wives were guarded because they were to bear the heirs to family wealth.

Sons had to concentrate on making that wealth. Any sign of sexual interest or activity was suppressed in their youth. Sexuality and love had to take second place to economic interests, and the marriages of young men, like those of their sisters, had to serve the family's ambitions.

In this kind of family life, sexuality was not supposed to be visible. It was veiled with Victorian prudery—as the rebellious generation of the 1920s would call it. Live-in servants, who were chiefly women, were expected to be celibate. To be a "maid" meant to be an unmarried maiden, as well as a servant. Pregnancy was hidden. Certain topics and words could not be mentioned in polite company. At dinner, one asked for "white meat" rather than breast of chicken. Even the legs of pianos were covered in a "proper" home. All this modesty kept sexuality and pleasure in the background, repressed in the interest of productive goals.

In this atmosphere, tensions naturally arose around sexuality and the power of the husband and father. They were suppressed in the family, but they found an outlet in art and science by the end of the nineteenth century. Plays such as Henrik Ibsen's *A Doll's House* exposed women's resentment about their passive, doll-like lives. Sigmund Freud developed psychoanalysis, a therapy to release repressed emotions. His upper-middle-class patients, he found, were suffering in adult life from the sexual feelings they had not been allowed to express in early childhood. Today Freud himself is criticized for some of his patriarchal notions. Yet his work contributed to a powerful critique of the patriarchal family life of his time. Repressed feelings of love may be necessary to sustain family authority, but they lead to symptoms of mental distress that Freud called neurosis.

Working-class families also became nuclear with industrialization, but there is a great difference between them and families of the bourgeoisie. Everyone in a working-class family had to work.[18] In the early 1900s, only a third of foreign-born families in the United States could live on the wages of a male "head." Most young children worked on the land or did odd jobs in the towns. They ran errands, peddled things, tended store, took care of still younger children, and helped their mothers doing piecework at home. At ten and twelve (and routinely at as young as five in nineteenth-century England and the United States), they went into mines, factories, and sweatshops.

These girls and boys were part of the wage-earning labor force. They worked as hard and as long as adult men. But in the mines and mills, the highest-paying jobs were reserved for the men. Children and women never earned enough to live on. They were used as unskilled workers, had the lowest rates of pay, and often worked the longest hours. They also worked in unhealthy and unsafe conditions. Young children labored long hours underground in the mines. Others spent all the daylight hours in mills, and accidents were frequent because workers were not protected from dangerous machinery. The labor laws that were meant to protect young children and women from such abuses came late, and only after a great deal of struggle. In 1908, the minimum age for child labor in the United States was set at ten years, and health and safety standards for children began to be imposed. Gradually, compulsory schooling also reduced child labor. Protective legislation was extended to women workers, too, but there were no laws to secure equal work or pay for women until the 1960s and 1970s.

Because wages were so low among industrial workers, family life was a means of survival as well as a source of affection and human warmth in lives brutalized by poverty. Only by pooling their wages could working-class people hope to feed and house themselves. Youths and immigrants who came to the cities alone usually moved in with other families, as in the days of the preindustrial household. Now, however, they went out to work and paid for their room and board with money rather than labor. Since wages gave them freedom to move, they were less subject to patriarchal tyranny than apprentices and servants had been in the preindustrial household.

Thus girls and boys, young women and men, went to work outside the home. In this major sense, the working-class family differed from that of the owning class. Yet there was a similarity between the two groups in the family's division of labor. In both kinds of families, most mothers remained based in the home.

(text continued on page 26)

Families Throughout History

Although human beings always seem to form families, the nature of those families varies from society to society and has changed over time. Even within the same culture, different groups of people form different kinds of families. Patterns of child rearing, of who lives with whom, and of how work is divided are quite diverse. Family members may work together, doing piecework at home or laboring in the fields; they may have one or two family members "go out" to earn income, leaving others to work in the home for no remuneration. Top left: a well-to-do family in the nineteenth century. Bottom left: a working-class family making toy animals at home. Right: a slave family picking cotton, near Savannah, Georgia, c. 1861.

Working-class mothers often needed to earn wages as their husbands' pay was usually low. Sometimes their husbands were sick, disabled, or unemployed. Some mothers became widows or were abandoned. But working-class mothers were handicapped in earning a living. The care of children claimed their time. And if they returned to waged work, they had to suffer the low pay and long hours allotted to women and still care for their families when they got home. Employers, unions, the fact that society made individual mothers solely responsible for children, all kept married women out of the labor force. As late as 1920, 90 percent of the female labor force in the United States was made up of single women.[19] How many of them merely claimed to be single we do not know. Nor do we know how many were forced to remain single so as to support parents and other family members.

Keeping married women out of factories, offices, and even schools did not keep them from working for pay, however. It simply bound them to unskilled, underpaid, and unpaid work in the home and outside it. Married women took in boarders and did piecework at home for textile factories and laundries. They did other people's sewing, laundry, and housework. And aside from whatever "productive" work they did for pay, the primary job of working-class mothers was unpaid child care and housework.

Like the ladies of the bourgeoisie, the working-class mother took care of her family's reproductive and consuming needs. That is, she did the necessary cleaning, shopping, cooking, child care, and nurturing to maintain her family. Attending to those tasks in the home without servants was a full-time job. And increasingly, as the twentieth century progressed, the homes of the middle class, like the homes of the working class, were without servants. Most women did most of the work of maintaining their families themselves.

Women's Work in the Home. In the industrialized United States, until as late as the 1970s, the majority of married women worked exclusively in their own homes. Despite changes in technology and different levels of family income, most twentieth-century mothers have spent their days doing housework and caring for the children and whatever other relatives live in the home.

Housework is a catchall term that covers a number of tasks done at home. Obtaining food is one aspect of housework. For some families, food raising is still a part of household work. Historically, the more men did socially organized wage work, the more women and children became responsible for the farming, gardening, raising of chickens, and so forth that supplied some of the family's food. This happens when the family still owns or rents some land. As urban life grew at the expense of rural life, however, food was bought rather than raised. Then shopping became a basic part of housekeeping.

Cleaning, preparing, cooking, and serving food in the form of meals call for different skills. Contemporary housewives report that next to child rearing, they like cooking most among their various tasks. It is creative and is usually appreciated. Cleaning up after meals, cleaning the home so that it is orderly and usable, keeping the furnishings and clothing of the family in good condition (and in an earlier time, making cloth and clothing), make up yet another complex of jobs. As skills, laundering, ironing, and mending bear little relation to each other, or to housecleaning, and many housewives say they are not particularly satisfying tasks. They are monotonous, because they are constantly repeated and never completed. And they are generally not appreciated. This work is noticed only when it is *not* done—when a shirt is missing a button, a bed not made, a floor not clean.

Add child care to housework, and we begin to see why the job of "housewife," according to a study done in the 1970s, takes an average of seventy-seven hours a week.[20] Most housewives who have been surveyed say that child rearing is the most rewarding part of their work. They also speak of the conflicts it sets up with the other demands of housework and of life in general. The care of children has little in common with housekeeping—except that in nuclear family arrangements, both are carried out in the private home, usually by the same person: the mother. Child care requires a set of skills and interests that are sometimes directly opposed to those required by housekeeping—and by husband care. Should one keep the floors clean or let the children play? Does one follow the rhythms of young life or force children into the schedule of a working father?

Moreover, not every woman has the attitudes and interests child care calls for, or can sustain an interest in children all day long, day after day. Infants need and have a right to close attention, feeding, fondling, changing, and stimulation for play and learning. Young children also need and deserve loving attention to their bodily, emotional, and imaginative needs. Some mothers are fully satisfied with their daily work in the home. Others have conflicting feelings. They enjoy their children, but feel the loneliness that child care in the isolated home imposes. They sometimes speak of the despair that overtakes them as they face the daily routine of endless caring for others with no time for their own needs. The resentment and guilt that build up often create unhappiness.

Over a hundred years ago, an English feminist pointed out that there was no good reason to expect that every mother enjoyed, or was even particularly good at, meeting children's daily needs. It was also wasteful, Harriet Taylor Mill wrote, to require each and every married woman to stay in her home all day with her children. Women who really enjoyed children could set up a nursery for several such families. This would free the energies of those who might have other talents and interests.

Harriet Taylor also noticed that child rearing in the private home by the mother was coercive. That is, mothers had no choice in the matter, because there were no other socially acceptable arrangements. On the one hand, society said it was "natural" for married women to stay at home and care for children. And on the other hand, society refused to employ married women, or even educate them so as to fit them for other jobs. If full-time mothering was so natural, she queried, why did it have to be enforced this way? Why were there prejudices and even laws against educating women, and about employing mothers, if they "naturally" took to staying at home with children?

Of course, there is nothing natural about any way of raising children, or those ways would not be so varied. Social custom, not nature, determines what mothering means. Well into the eighteenth century, for example, the aristocratic upper classes of Europe sent their infants to wetnurses until they were weaned at three or four. Urban women who worked as silk spinners and artisans did the same.[21] The wetnurse was usually a peasant who had just recently given birth herself and had a nursing baby of her own. She took in one, and sometimes more, babies and nursed them—as women in the preindustrial household did—while carrying out her work and life in the countryside. Ironically, even among the nineteenth-century bourgeoisie—the group from which we inherit the idea that women are chiefly mothers—the reality was quite different from the ideology. Affluent women of this period frequently handed over the care of their children to servants or slaves—the nannies, governesses, and black mammies who did the daily work of mothering.

Men's participation in child care also varies in different cultures and different eras. In tribal societies, a network of female and male kin often care for each others' children. They are all "daughters" and "sons," looked after by the entire group. Among the Arapesh of New Guinea, Margaret Mead observed that the father as well as the mother is said to "bear a child." The father as well as the mother stays with the infant and meets its momentary needs. Both father and mother are held responsible for child care by the entire community. Indeed, she goes on to say, "if one comments upon a middle-aged man as good-looking, the people answer: 'Good-looking? Ye-e-s? But you should have seen him before he bore all those children.' "[22]

What? Men give birth? That may be a little too remote from our experience, although several societies have such notions. What is familiar from our preindustrial period, however, is that fathers were closely involved in the daily work of raising children. The father's role in the preindustrial household included teaching and disciplining. He particularly trained the boys of the household in their future work skills. When fathers left the home to work in factories and offices, the sexual division of labor with regard to child rearing was sharpened. Compulsory schooling took over many of the father's tasks. This brought the benefit of literacy to children, but it meant that fathers lost control over training the boys of the family. It also meant that care of younger children fell almost entirely to women, especially to mothers, who were becoming ever more isolated as everyone else left the home each day for school or for wage work.

Nursing makes up a final set of tasks that has been assigned to women in the home. Until the development in the twentieth century of hospitals and nursing homes as places of treatment and care, even great ladies were supposed to care for the ill of their household, including servants and slaves. As with child care, however, servant women did the most difficult physical tasks of nursing. Today people get much of their medical and nursing care outside the home. But such care is expensive. It is not available to everyone. Thousands of rural communities in the United States lack even one doctor, and they do not have systems of transportation to any medical care. Even in cities, health care is often unavailable or too costly for most low-income families. When this is the case, nursing still falls to the wife and mother. Indeed, it is often regarded as one of her duties even when a family can afford professional care. Families expect to be nursed by mother, even though today's mother does not have the help of relatives in the home, any more than she has servants.

Combine nursing—which also includes attending to the emotional needs of all family members—with the demands of child care and the chores of housework, and we can see why "a woman's work is never done." What is harder to understand, is why people also say that housewives "don't work."

The tasks performed by the housewife are necessary, time-consuming work. One of the main reasons housework is so time-consuming is that it remained private while other work was socially organized. Studies conducted in three countries show that, despite household appliances, the hours spent on housework have not decreased from 1929 to the 1970s.[23] The housewife does not get paid for these hours of work. She does not charge for the meals, housecleaning, laundered clothing, and nursing she provides, any more than she charges for child care. And because she is not paid, her work does not get economic recognition. This sometimes makes it seem as though she doesn't work at all. Yet, clearly, she does work that *can* be paid for.[24] For pay, a housekeeper or a team of housecleaners can do the family's housecleaning—and they do, in certain income groups. With higher family income, restaurants or a hired cook can provide meals. Laundries, dry cleaners, and tailors can take care of furnishings and clothes. Although these paid services may not be ideal substitutes for the unpaid work of housewives, they enable us to measure the real costs of housework.

The reason housewives have not been paid is because they are the last group in industrial society to do their work in their homes. No member of the preindustrial household was paid for labor. The household simply housed, fed, and clothed them. Only apprentices and live-in workers earned some small pay, and even they worked mostly for room, board, and training. No one worked just for wages until labor was socially organized outside the home. But then, only those who went out to work got that wage.

Through the late nineteenth and into the twentieth century, working men in factory after factory organized to demand a "family wage." This wage was meant to support *all* the necessary work of the family. It was to take the place of the property once owned by the individual household. Since working families could no longer own the property now needed for their work— the mines, the factories, the machines—since they could no longer raise their own food, or sell the products of their labor, the family wage supplied the means of subsistence for a family unit. The family wage was distributed very unevenly, however. Only organized workers in certain skilled occupations received it, and they, by definition, were adult males.

Women had to continue in the pattern we have described— whether they were the few supported by the family wage of a husband, or the many who were not. Single, they could not earn enough to live independently. And married, they could not hold on to decent, full-time jobs outside the home. A married woman had little choice but to do all the work that remained to be done in the home. That work enabled her husband and the older children to go to their jobs every morning. But since they got the wage that supported her labors in the home, it seemed to pay for their work only. Thus, housewives were—and are—said to do their seventy-seven hours a week labor just "for love."

If women who worked in their homes were paid, even at one dollar an hour, we would begin to appreciate their labor. We would notice that housewives work—and for longer hours, less pay, and none of the benefits of the male wage earner. The conditions of work in the home would become clear, along with the attitudes women, men, and children have toward it—and each other. As of now, the housewife is always on call to serve the family's "needs" for comfort, service, and care. On the one hand, it is her job, so no one is expected to perform these services for her. On the other hand, it is no job at all—so along with no pay, she gets no days off, no vacation, and no retirement. Today, even married women employed outside the home do about forty hours a week of housework. That is ten times more than married men do, in the care of what is also *their* home and children.[25]

This, then, is how the nuclear family emerged from the preindustrial household. Socially organized production changed the quality of family life, as well as of work. With most kinds of work done outside the home, families came to depend on wages, rather than their own property, for the necessities of life. And as capital squeezed out household property, the household master lost his position, too. He was no longer master of his economic fate. He was still master in the home, however. Only the bourgeois husband and father continued to own property that supported his wife and children at home and at school. Yet working-class people also experienced the division of labor that marked the new, bourgeois economic order. In the work force, adult men—although often impoverished, exploited, and unemployed themselves—nonetheless earned wages consistently higher than youths and women. And in the family, although mothers and children also worked, they were dependent upon the wage of an adult male as their main means of subsistence. The family thus continued as a patriarchal, economic unit.

Although families no longer work together in a household, they still form households—residences in which the income and labor of all the members are pooled. As families, they carry out the tasks necessary for social life. Their work in home, factory, and office has been reorganized by industrial, capitalist society; but families still work to sustain themselves and raise the next generation.

It was out of these historical developments—the introduction of wage work and the division of family labor—that our image of the ideal family arose. Daddy leaves the home to go to work. Mommy stays home cooking and cleaning. And there are Dick and Jane at school, learning skills and attitudes that will fit them for the work their mother and father do. Yet we know that this is not a true picture of all family life—not in the past, and certainly not now. Today, something is happening to the nuclear family which is exciting and disturbing. It is affecting us all.

Family and Sex Roles in Flux

A striking change is taking place in the United States in patterns of family life. Over the last twenty years, the "traditional" nuclear family has become less and less typical. Today, the nuclear family with father working outside the home and mother and children at home "not working" can hardly be regarded as the norm.

As we have seen, this "ideal" nuclear family was never quite what it seemed to be. Even in families of higher-paid skilled workers and professionals, who came closest to living according to the nuclear family ideal, women's work in the home helped support the family. Women and children were dependent on the father's wage, however. This obscured the fact that father and children were also dependent on mother's work in the home. And it made schooling seem like a gift, rather than a new form of training for work in industrial society. In many other families, the discrepancy between the real and the ideal was even more striking. Where fathers earned less money, children held jobs after school and ended their schooling early to be able to work full-time. Married women, especially in new immigrant groups and among racial minorities, earned money, if only at low-paying, part-time jobs. And, of course, some adults lived alone, some lived with children in single-parent families, and some lived as unmarried couples.

Today, however, only 7 to 15 percent of American families fit into the nuclear family norm of father at work and mother at home with the children.[26] Two major developments account for this fact. One is the dramatic increase of married women in the work force. The other is equally dramatic but less evident—the growing number of adults who live in households without children. These changes in work and population patterns are closely related, and both lead to a new sense of the relations between children and parents, women and men, families and society.

Mother Has a Paying Job. Women now make up about half the labor force in the United States. And where married women were only 10 percent of the female labor force in 1920, that figure rose in 1976 to 75 percent. The great increase in women workers has been among married women, particularly among mothers.[27]

Half of all mothers of school-age children are wage earners in the United States today.[28] The reason has to do in part with the continued organization of work outside the home. The same development of socially organized production that made men wage earners is now making wage earners out of women, mothers included. On the one hand, the steadily rising costs of clothing, food, housing, schooling, nursing, and health care that can no longer be provided by the household make mothers seek paying jobs. And on the other hand, jobs open up as the goods and services that women once provided in the home come to be commercially made and sold. Now, as ever, women generally work because they cannot afford not to. But now, even when they are married, they—like men—work full-time for wages outside the home.

The entry of married women into the labor force has had profound effects upon family and sexual arrangements. These effects are being felt by almost everyone. They are not just private matters. Nor are they temporary. Married women are apparently in the labor force to stay.[29] They need to be there if their families are to survive. Yet married women cannot work outside the home without other changes taking place. Who cares for children—and who cares for adults? These become urgent questions, and they call for social as well as personal responses.

The care of children is a major social concern as well as a family one. Children are essential if a society is to survive. Yet our society has not found ways to provide loving, educational surroundings for millions of children whose parents are working outside the home. By 1976, 37 percent of mothers who had children under six were employed. At the same time, only 1.7 percent of the 16 million children of wage-earning mothers found places in child-care centers.[30] Where were all the other children? Some were cared for at home by other relatives or by paid child-care workers. Some were cared for in other people's homes. And some were home without any care at all. The quality of such care in the home (or lack of it) is very varied.

Families that most need the mother's income are the ones least able to pay for the nurseries and centers that are available. Publicly supported child-care centers are rare. Government, which is in charge of public funds, has not assumed this responsibility in the United States as it has in other countries, such as Sweden. Nor has industry, which employs workers and sets their rates of pay. There seems to be a great reluctance on the part of these powerful social institutions to meet the physical, emotional, and intellectual needs of the next generation.

Moreover, some parents object to child rearing outside the home. Others, however, argue for the benefits of rearing small groups of children together, under the guidance of supportive adults. They also see child care outside the home as an opportunity to have men as well as women care for young children. But those who oppose nursery and day-care centers fear that children cared for by others will not feel they "belong" to their families. They fear depersonalized, noncaring situations— which can in fact come about when lack of funds and support make nurseries mere baby-sitting centers.

Since mothers are working outside the home because they must, however—and ever more will be doing so—someone has to take care of children. Perhaps fears about nurseries and day care can be met by demanding *good* child-care arrangements. Working families clearly need nurseries and child-care centers. Public and/or employer-funded centers should be made available. Yet families could still oversee the kind of care their children receive. These centers could be made as accountable to parents as the costly private ones are.

As more married women enter the labor force, relations between the sexes also change. These changes are causing controversy, too. In part the problems that arise have to do with work. When both parents work outside the home, there is a need—on women's part, at least—for a fairer sharing of what remains of housekeeping and child care in the home. It is not simply unjust for one of the parties who works all day to shop, prepare dinner, clean up, care for the home, and care for the children. It is physically draining and emotionally abusive, too.

Sharing family work may seem fair and logical and be threatening nonetheless. Girls and boys have been brought up expecting women to be economically dependent on men. The norm was for men to bring in the income. Women were expected to be inept at business and politics, poor at figures—but emotionally supportive of husbands and children. They lacked authority, but they were supposed to be "naturally" good at the domestic work that served their family's needs.

The family's division of labor has been the greatest shaper of sex roles. Generations of children have learned to relate to each other in terms of mommy and daddy's pattern of behavior—or what it was *supposed to* have been. They learned to become feminine and masculine, according to the nuclear family norm. Women were "feminine" if and only if they did women's work in the home. Males who did such work were ridiculed. School and work reinforced the family's division of labor and paternal authority as well. Sports, mathematics, engineering, law, and business were male pursuits. Reading, nursing, teaching elementary school, and clerical work were for women. The labor force reflects this pattern even today. Women are employed at low-paying, sex-segregated jobs. They earn only 60 percent of what men earn. And women almost always report to male bosses.

Today, women make up about half the nation's paid workforce. Will society continue to cling to the idea of "woman's place" and resist what we might well call mothers' rights? Most women still become mothers. Since almost half the mothers of the United States work for pay, they are surely right to demand access to all kinds of jobs, and wages equal to men's. In 1980, their pay is low, their working conditions poor, and their job status inferior. As long as we insist that the old norm still holds, and that mother's place is in the home, the *real* situation of mothers suffers. Indeed, the situation of all women—and of the families they work to support—suffers. Employers rely on the old nuclear family ideal to keep women's wages low. Since "normally" women are supported by men, employers argue, why should they expect a fair wage?

Children, men, even women may cooperate in this myth—for fear of what equality between women and men might mean. If women are full agents in society, their role as perpetual motherers will have to change. But does this mean that women and men will form a sharing relation in the family, whereby they both serve each other and their children? Everyone is afraid of losing something familiar in gaining this new equality—even if the familiar now conflicts with family needs. Both children and men can gain a great deal if fathers participate fully in child rearing. With women earning money, men lose the burden of sole responsibility for the income of the family. But men also lose the service and patriarchal authority that went with their economic power. Women may have ambivalent feelings about shared parenting. On the one hand, they do not want always to be the only person children turn to; on the other hand, that role offers some satisfactions. And by gaining equality, women also lose the right that minors have, to be dependent.

Divorce, which now ends one of every three marriages (and one of every two first marriages), may reflect these new pressures in part. Many women who resent an unfair division of family work and authority are now economically able to change their status. Divorce does not seem to threaten the family as an institution, since most divorces lead to remarriage. The high divorce rate seems rather to point to a need many people feel to restructure their marital relations.

Equal work and responsibility in the family means that girls and boys, men and women, will have to learn to relate to each other differently outside the home, too. They will no longer be boss and helper. They will be teammates, co-workers, and voices of equal authority. Such changes in status and power affect everything—from who makes the beds and changes the diapers to who governs the country and sits in judgment in the high courts of the land.

A Longer and More Varied Life. There are other important reasons, in addition to mothers working outside the home, for changes in family life. Changes in family size, life expectancy, marriage, contraception, and divorce also make families depart from the old norm. And they, too, give rise to needs and practices that are new and controversial.

The move toward smaller family size in a way defines the nuclear family. As the household ceased to be a center of production in the nineteenth and twentieth centuries, the family, in the sense of who lives in the home, had to become smaller. Those who once found work in the household and on its land had to leave it to find wage work. Only the nuclear core of the preindustrial household remained—consisting of parents and children. This change in the composition of the household occurred gradually. At first, workers lodged with families near their place of work and paid for room and board. Around 1900, in urban centers such as New York City, only 50 percent of the households of working people were made up of just the nuclear core.[31] But the "exodus of adults" from the family, as it has been called, continued. Fewer and fewer homes continued to hold a widowed grandparent, a maiden aunt, unmarried adult children, or an unrelated lodger. These are people who live alone today. From just 1940 to 1970, there was a 12 percent decline in family size—and three-quarters of that decline was due to the shrinking number of adults in the family.[32] Young adults leave home earlier, before they are married. Older ones continue to live alone after the death of a spouse.

Along with this kind of reduction in family size, families are also having fewer children. This development is a further reason for making us question why mothers should be confined to the home. It contradicts the nineteenth-century definition of woman's role as lifelong mother. Mothers now have fewer children, and have them more closely spaced, than ever in history. Families need, for their 1.8 children per family, only two to four years of infant care.

The declining birthrate is connected with changes in mortality (death rate). So is the increase in divorce. The frequent death of children and adults down to the middle of the nineteenth century made for family patterns very different from our own. Marriages, for example, lasted from twelve to seventeen years for the preindustrial peasantry of Europe. People entered their first marriages later than we do. They had to wait until they had enough property to start a household. Many people without property did not marry at all. Women who did marry, were twenty-four or twenty-five years old in eighteenth-century England and France. Men were about twenty-seven. Such couples seldom lived long enough to raise their children to adulthood. After about fifteen years of marriage, one of the parents would die, usually the mother in childbirth. That first marriage would be followed by a second, and the raising of a second family.

This meant that most children lost at least one parent as they were growing up. Many of them would be raised in households with stepparents, half-brothers and sisters, and perhaps with some orphaned cousins, too. Preindustrial society was more youthful than our own. Mortality was very high among infants and children, so more children had to be born to replenish the adult world. In seventeenth-century England, for example, one-quarter to one-third of all the children born died before they were fifteen. In one well-to-do family, the wife, who had married at nineteen, bore twenty-one children before her husband died. Yet only four daughters and one son survived her.[33]

Today most people marry young. Wage-earning couples do not have to wait until they inherit the family land or shop, or save up a dowry. At the same time, life expectancy has almost doubled. The death rate in Europe and the United States is down to about one-third of what it was in the eighteenth century.[34] Changes such as these explain why families are now choosing how long to stay married, and how many children to raise. Death no longer decides these matters for us.

Today's pattern of divorce and remarriage actually recreates the marriage pattern of preindustrial families. It seems to be less disruptive to the family life of children, however, than the old pattern of death and remarriage. The percentage of children under fourteen who lose a parent by death or divorce has been decreasing. In the United States, that number fell from 27.8 percent in 1900 to 19.1 percent in 1978. The total percentage of children who live in families with at least one of their natural parents is also increasing.[35] Wage work does away with the preindustrial practice of fostering, sending out children to other households. And it now permits women to raise children on their own if they need or want to.

The declining birthrate, like divorce, is another response to changes in life expectancy. Modern nutrition, sanitation, and medicine have dramatically reduced the death rate among infants and children. This is less true for the poor in the United States and throughout the world, where malnutrition and lack of health care still claim the lives of many children. In general, however, most children who are born in industrialized countries now live to adulthood. And now that death does not limit the number of children families can raise, families tend to limit the number of births.

The reduction of births has been made easier, yet more controversial, by the technology of mass contraception. Almost all societies have sought to limit (or increase) their numbers in relation to their resources. Some of their methods seem inhumane to us. Eskimos let aged parents perish, for example. In ancient Greece, Arabia, and in Nepal until very recently, female infanticide was widely practiced. Today's contraceptive technology can resolve some of the problems other societies have faced, but it raises many problems of its own. Women's groups and health groups are very critical of the dangerous side effects of the most widely used female contraceptives. Some religious denominations oppose abortion, and some oppose all forms of contraception. Other groups representing poor women and racial minorities argue that lack of public funds for family

planning coerces such women to accept sterilization. Sterilization, which is publicly funded, is irreversible, whereas contraception and abortion permit continued choice.[36]

Here as elsewhere in matters concerning the family, there' is
conflict, controversy, and change. While most people who have
been surveyed support the right of women themselves to choose
if and when they will bear a child,[37] other groups and many laws
still oppose this. At the same time, there are new reasons for
limiting birth today. In addition to changed mortality rates and
the cost of raising children in an advanced industrial society,
there is the question of the relation of the world's people to its
resources. Some argue that births should be drastically reduced
where resources are scarce. Others point out, however, that food
and other necessities simply need to be fairly distributed.
Actually, it is now economically possible for all children who are
born to live and thrive. It is economically possible for all to have
the food, health care, housing, and education they need. The
potential is there for a humane and socially just control of birth
and death—if social policy is geared to a fair distribution of
resources and to the rights of women to bear as well as not
to bear.

Whatever one's moral position on birth control, the fact of its
spreading use is socially important. Changes in patterns of life
and death, modern modes of work, awareness of the need to
distribute the world's resources fairly—all account for today's
smaller families, as does the will of women and families to
exercise choice in having children and in spacing births. The
desire to limit births, and the ability to do so, in turn affects our
notions about sexuality. Indeed, much of the opposition to
contraception and abortion has to do with this. There is fear that
birth control will disrupt the bond between sexuality, marriage,
and family.

It is important, in dealing with this issue, to notice that the
declining birthrate affects how many children will be raised in a
family, *not* how many people will be parents. If anything, more
people get married today, and become parents, than ever before.
Preindustrial society kept entire groups of people unmarried—
sons and daughters with no inheritance; apprentices, servants,

and journeyman; spinners (spinsters) in textile centers; soldiers, prostitutes, monks, nuns, and priests. Yet sexuality was more tightly bound to family and marriage than it need be today. It is possible today for women and men to lead lives together without raising children. It is economically possible, and birth control makes it biologically possible, too. Since this does not threaten the social order as it did when society was founded upon the patriarchal household, the childless family and the unmarried couple living together have become more acceptable. The same is true for lesbian or male homosexual couples. Women also are now more able to raise children in single-parent families or in collective households.

Such changes in sexual patterns and living arrangements are social facts today. They are part of the context within which we make our moral choices. Even though society is particularly slow in accepting departures from the norm in regard to sexuality, options are now opening for those who have no wish to live in nuclear family arrangements. Neither marriage, parenting, nor raising children in a family is on the decline. But those who wish to live otherwise are able to move a little more openly into alternative family situations.

One final, but major, alternative pattern has yet to be mentioned. It ultimately affects most people, and it is one of the chief reasons why only 7 to 15 percent of today's families fit the old norm. What has been called the most radical change in the twentieth-century American family is how long parents now live alone after their children leave home. Couples who now marry at twenty and twenty-one tend to have few children, to have them soon after marriage, and to space them closely. That means they are in their early forties when their children start living on their own. This is a family situation almost all of us will face. Yet it is one our society has barely begun to reckon with. It is a new pattern—parents living out long lives of their own without children, and continuing to live on, often alone, after the death of a spouse.

Almost half the people who live alone today are over sixty-five. They are retired, often against their wishes. That means they are isolated from social networks that work generally provides, and they live on reduced incomes. Families, who could once give social and economic support to their elders, no longer have the resources to do so. Wage-earning families do not have space to house aging parents, relatives, or friends. They do not have family members at home to attend them. Nor do most families any longer need the abilities and skills of older people. Many middle-aged people will feel anguish and guilt toward the older generation, in the belief that families somehow should provide the space, time, and attention their elders deserve— when, in fact, they cannot. As with child care, new social arrangements are called for. Ties of affection between the generations are probably as strong as ever, but traditional modes of family care have broken down—and new modes have yet to emerge.

Like children in today's society, older people are victims of the most recent changes in the nuclear family. It is as though the present, ever more nucleated form of family life serves only those who work, or are being trained to do so. The family, for them, is a residential unit. It is the primary unit for consumption and reproduction. It is the unit within which we find affection and support. But the numbers of people we can extend that family support to are shrinking. Our very young and our old need some new connective tissue to bind them to society and give them vital support. They, and perhaps all of us, are in need of some sustaining social associations—age-integrated sport and cultural centers, local health and nursing centers, neighborhood gardening groups, block associations, self-help groups—networks to mediate between the wage-earning family and the work-oriented society it is now so dependent upon.

Loss of the old nuclear family norm does not mean the end of the family, or even of the nuclear family. It does mean that our development as a society has carried us beyond what we once viewed as normal, or ideal, patterns of family life. Some of those patterns were more myths than realities, as we saw. The major flaw in the notion of the ideal nuclear family was that it made children and women appear idle, as if they no longer took part in the necessary work of society as they had in the days of the preindustrial household. Actually, all that had changed were the modes of work. Adult male labor outside the home was recognized and waged. The schooling of children that replaced apprenticeship was not. Nor was the work of women in the home. Since neither children nor women received wages, it seemed as though they did not work. Yet without their labor, the work force could not be sustained or replaced.

Steadily, however, married women and mothers were drawn into the paid work force, too. It is increasingly necessary now for mothers to work outside the home to support themselves and their families. But because child rearing in the private home has not been viewed as socially necessary work, no social provisions have been made for care of preschool children or for older children after school hours. This is one of the urgent, unresolved problems of our time.

Women and men are also experiencing strains because of the sex roles assigned to them in terms of the old nuclear family ideal. As women gain economic independence, they seek to equalize relations between the sexes. Men feel new pressures to take on their share of family work. It is clear that men lose some of their old patriarchal prerogatives as they lose sole control of the family's resources. On the other hand, there are new possibilities for democratic family relations and for shared responsibilities. The course our society will take here is not yet certain.

Other developments that carry family life beyond the old norm have to do with changes in family size, life expectancy, marriage, and divorce. The frequency of divorce, and the fact that there are fewer children in today's families, sometimes make it seem as though the family is disappearing as an institution. Yet these signs of fragile family life prove deceptive, as we saw, when placed in historical perspective. More children then ever in recent history are now reared within their families by at least one of their natural parents. What has changed here is simply that lower mortality rates for infants, children, and adults now make possible choices about family size and duration of marriage that people did not have before.

Making such choices raises conflicts with traditional values, however. Divorce and contraception are far from universally accepted, for example, even though they are becoming more widespread. There is also controversy over, and a growing acceptance of, alternate family arrangements. All these developments emerge from new patterns of work and population changes, but they raise problems nonetheless. It is a little like the potential we now have for longer, more varied lives—a potential that confronts us, at the same time, with a need for new social forms if we are to realize it in creative, fulfilling ways.

Every generation has to find its own way of shaping its institutions. But perhaps having surveyed the past—having seen the great variety of family forms humans have devised, and the reasons for the evolution of our own—we may have a surer sense of the social possibilities and problems before us.

TWO: The Family Tree

Contemporary Patterns in the United States

By Renate Bridenthal

WHAT IS A FAMILY TODAY? When people are living during a time of rapid change, they sometimes do not recognize new patterns. In the case of the family, new combinations are emerging, even though many people still think of the family as mother, father, and a few children. Is a mother alone with several children a family? Are two women or men living together with the children of one or both of them one family, two families, or a shared household? Is a woman living with her adult daughter's child and her own adult son a family or a broken family? And what about a childless couple? The answer to these questions will depend on how traditional a view one has of the family and how well one understands its changing formations. Newspapers, magazines, books, and television keep looking at "the state of the family," measuring its health, and reporting various conclusions. Some fear that it is falling apart, others think not. These judgments are often based on how observers define what a family is. Depending on the definition, one can see families today persisting or dissolving, or perhaps just transforming—moving in a new direction and taking on a new shape. So the term itself must be examined and its meaning established.

What Is a Family?

The U.S. Bureau of the Census defines a family as a household of two or more individuals related by blood or by law. Such a broad definition can take in most people. In 1977, 90 percent of the population lived in such households, down only slightly from a high of 94 percent in 1960.[1] The other 10 percent were living either alone; in households with unrelated persons; or in institutions like hospitals, prisons, orphanages, and old-age homes. Judging from this statistic, one could argue that the family is here to stay.[2] On the other hand, the Census Bureau definition conceals the fact that many families are shrinking in size down to a simple twosome of single parent and child, couple without children, or couple with grown children living away from home. Such families were, until recently, thought of as "broken" or "remnants."

Although the Census definition includes these twosomes, it does not consider the "extended" family, that is, the continuing blood relationships outside the household of a core family—the grandparents or cousins, for example. After all, people may live apart and still feel "family." In fact, it seems that household and family are not always the same thing. People may share a household and not consider themselves a family, and people may feel like family while not living together. Since living together is a particular form of closeness, however, its trends are important and get noticed.

The debate about the future of the family has grown so heated and complicated that a 1975 definition in the *Journal of Home Economics*, a journal in a field of study concerned mainly with preserving the family, leaves out all mention of residence or of biological or legal relationship among family members. "Family," says the journal, "is defined as a unit of intimate, transacting, and interdependent persons who share some values and goals, resources, responsibility for decisions, and have commitment to one another over time."[3] This is an even looser definition than that of the Census Bureau. It includes people who previously would not have been considered a family. Are we just keeping the word alive?

Permanence is another feature that is supposed to distinguish family from "mere" friendship. But this, too, is a distortion created by longing for a past that may never have existed. In the past, early death frequently rearranged families. Today, death comes much later, and so families may be seen as actively rearranging their lives through divorce and remarriage. Many contemporary individuals will live in a number of different

families. Imagine one person's possible family experi
child begins with an original set of parents. Should th
separate, the child moves into another home as
twosome, usually with the mother, but sometimes
father. If that parent takes another partner, the child then joins
another family and may visit the other biological parent on
weekends. Soon, our imaginary child may have a new half-
brother or half-sister, or perhaps one from each original parent.
Now suppose this child grows up and establishes a similar
pattern. She or he might marry; get a divorce and live with a child
from the first marriage; then marry someone else who brings
children from a first marriage, thus forming yet another new
family.

According to the Census definition, this person has been
through at least seven families, with some overlapping members.
If this individual has also lived with people unrelated by blood or
law, she or he may have been part of other families, according to
the definition of the *Journal of Home Economics.* Some patterns
are even more complex, with different adults—a grandmother,
an uncle, a good friend—taking responsibility for a child at
different times, depending on need and ability to provide care.

Thus, while virtually everybody has at least one experience of
family, many do not experience its permanence. Because most
other social institutions, like work or school, are even more open
and shifting, one's family often feels relatively stable, even
"permanent." The expression "Blood is thicker than water"
reflects the notion that family is more binding than other
relationships. But blood is not glue, as the many changing
relationships also suggest. Family can mean a variety of people
sharing a variety of commitments and goals. Family is a way of
looking at people or experiencing them. It is an institution and
an idea that is periodically redefined.[4]

Family may not be forever, but it is certainly the most
persistent experience we have in our lives. We are shaped by it,
favorably and unfavorably, repeating early family experiences in
adulthood or deliberately avoiding them. More often than not,
people identify themselves by their families, which shows how
deeply felt those roots are.

Families differ according to social class, religion, racial and/or ethnic group, and geographic location. They are also different for people in different phases of their life cycle. But of all these differences, the most important one is the social class into which one is born. Here is the start one gets in life: the material base for one's life chances and for much of one's psychological outlook, too. Whether individuals are aware of it or not, they tend to follow the patterns of their social class for such things as age at marriage; number of children; ways of rearing children; and chances of a mother working outside the home. Indeed, families create individuals at least as much as individuals create families.

Understanding Social Class. But what exactly is social class? If this is the strongest influence on family, then to understand the family, one must understand class. There are several definitions of class, not all of them in agreement. One very broad and commonly used definition sets down basic distinctions:

> By class is meant two or more orders of people who are believed to be, and are accordingly ranked by the members of the community, in socially superior and inferior positions. Members of a class tend to marry within their own order, but the values of the society permit marriage up and down. A class system also provides that children are born into the same status as their parents. A class society distributes rights and privileges, duties and obligations, unequally among its inferior and superior grades.[5]

This definition focuses on the fact of inequality, with some people ranked higher or lower on a scale of shared values. It also indicates that people in such a system—which we should recognize as our own—do not have equal opportunity, since children inherit a position on that scale. However, the definition is incomplete. It does not tell us what the desirable goods of society are or who controls access to them, and it makes the scale look more static and permanent than it is. In fact, the relationships that form social class have changed over time.

The period since the industrial revolution has been marked by important changes in the ownership of capital wealth, that is, the wealth that produces wealth, such as factories and machinery, raw materials, land used for agriculture, and money used for investment. Capital wealth means productive wealth, not just personal possessions people use for themselves. It is the kind of wealth that affects the lives of others by creating or taking away jobs, moving industry from one place to another, stimulating new technology, affecting the environment, and so on. Today, about 700,000 households in the United States control more than half of this kind of wealth. The remaining 58 million households belong to families whose lives are affected by that control.[6] Within the controlling group—some call it the ruling class—it is mainly the adult men who actually exercise this power, thus reducing further the number of individuals in control.

How did such a concentration of wealth occur? Since the industrial revolution, owners have employed workers to whom they have paid wages. The value of the goods produced by the workers has been greater than the amount of money the workers have been paid. Therefore, owners collect the surplus as profit when they sell products. Over time, successful businessmen could drive out competitors. Former owners thus became employees or workers. These changes are still going on. Today, small firms often go out of business, and large corporations produce most of our goods and merge with one another to form giant corporations like Exxon or IBM. Most people in the United States today work for wages paid by owners and so contribute to the further accumulation of capital wealth for these few owners. While ordinary people own some stock, they are not part of the controlling class. The key to entrance into the ruling or upper class is owning a large enough amount of stock to have a voice in important corporate decisions.

Mobility is the term for upward or downward social and economic movement of individuals and their families *relative to* the movement of others. It is not *absolute* movement, nor is it a simple up or down. For example, a family may "move up" the social and economic ladder relative to where its grandparents stood, but if most other families are moving up faster, it may in fact be moving down, *relatively*. It is important to remember that the criteria for measuring upward or downward mobility are also changing. For example, white-collar work used to put some people high on the social ladder. However, office work has become more and more routinized. Secretaries, typists, file clerks, and stenographers make few important decisions and are rarely eligible for high posts. And the pay for office work is less than for some manual work, where unions have won better wages and working conditions. So it is not at all clear whether working in a clean office is, in fact, upward mobility for a son or daughter of a factory worker. Sometimes what looks like moving up is only keeping up, or not even that.

Seeing families as either owners of productive property or wage earners may be the best way of understanding their relationship to one another. But since the vast majority belong in the latter category, we need other ways of distinguishing among them. Also, some people and families are not in either group: professionals who charge a fee and are self-employed, for example. Finally, there is a subjective factor apart from hard data, which is the *feeling* people have about what class they belong to. When asked, most people say they belong to "the middle class." This is a confusing term. Historically, the term "middle class" described a new group of city dwellers (burghers or bourgeoisie) who stood midway between serfs and aristocracy in the old feudal hierarchy or ranking system. When these two legally defined groups became less important as capitalism replaced feudalism, the "middle class" became so broad as to include almost everybody. In reality, the upper part of this historical bourgeoisie is today's upper class, replacing the aristocracy that once controlled landed wealth. This group now controls productive wealth. Today, people usually use the term "middle class" to describe some level of material comfort and respectability. Often it is used synonymously with the popular notion of "average." Since "middle class" connotes respectability, which is important for self-esteem, even workers earning a below-average wage may describe themselves as middle class.

Probably the most useful criteria for distinguishing social class are income and assets. Using these criteria, one can construct a chart that allows one to visualize families in a hierarchy of resources available to them. The danger of using such a chart is that it looks somewhat more static than it is. In fact, income and assets do not tell the whole story about social class. Other factors that go into determining social class are the type of work done by family members and its prestige in the society; the source of income (wages or profits); the level of education and types of schools attended; and the family ancestry, meaning where families come from, how long they have been in the United States, and how long they have been wealthy (if they are).

In looking at categories of social class, it is also important to remember that people are not fixed in them and may move up and down, though rarely in big jumps. For our purposes, we have set some income "dividing lines" between classes in order to see the percentage of families within each class. In fact, the dividing lines are somewhat arbitrary. For example, although we define the upper middle class as those earning above $30,000, some families with incomes of $32,000 might be more appropriately labeled middle class, depending on the type of work done by family members, family ancestry, etc. Similarly, under certain circumstances, families earning $28,000 might be considered upper middle class. Frequently those families near the upper or lower income limits of their class have much in common with members of the class just above or just below them.

Keeping all these complexities in mind, the chart on page 54 gives an overall sense of income distribution in the United States.[7] It indicates that about 13 percent of all families earn more than $30,000 a year, and that, therefore, 87 percent of the population earn less than that. The vast majority of the top 13 percent have incomes between $30,000 and $50,000; only about 2.5 percent of all families, therefore, earn more than $50,000 a year. Another way to look at this most wealthy portion of the population is to see who controls capital wealth. Approximately 1.5 percent of families own 80 percent of all stocks in the United States.[8] We can call them the upper class. Through their assets, these families either own or control the major units of the economy. Their decisions about what is most profitable for them affects the rest of the population, or, to put it another way, their decisions about what is best for their families affect what happens to other families. Some examples of upper-class families

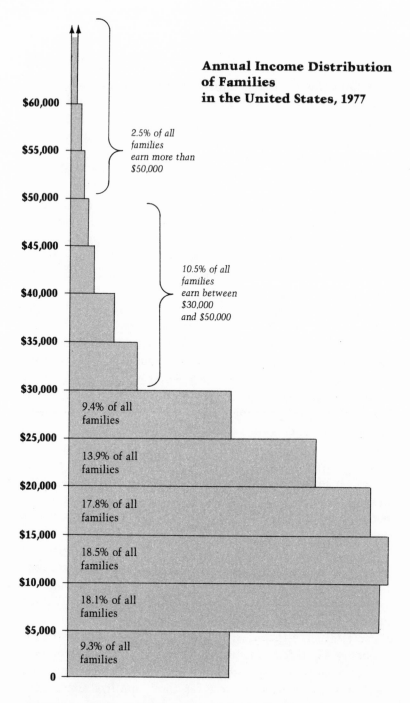

Annual Income Distribution of Families in the United States, 1977

$60,000

$55,000

2.5% of all families earn more than $50,000

$50,000

$45,000

$40,000

10.5% of all families earn between $30,000 and $50,000

$35,000

$30,000

9.4% of all families

$25,000

13.9% of all families

$20,000

17.8% of all families

$15,000

18.5% of all families

$10,000

18.1% of all families

$5,000

9.3% of all families

0

Note: 13% of all families earn more than $30,000; 41.1% earn between $15,000 and $30,000; 36.6% earn between $5,000 and $15,000.

are the Du Ponts (who control General Motors, U.S. Rubber, chemical companies); the Rockefellers (who control Standard Oil, Chase Manhattan Bank); the Mellons (who control Alcoa, Gulf Oil, the Mellon bank); and the Fords (who control Ford Motor Company and appliance companies). The actual annual income of each family member is secret, but it is somewhere between half a million and several million dollars. Each of David Rockefeller's six children has been willed a $25 million personal inheritance,[9] and David himself is only one of six children of the fortune's founder.

Upper-class families are not only very rich and powerful, but many of them have also been in the United States and have been wealthy for a long time. The farther back rich families go, the "better" they are considered; an ancestry going back to colonial times is ideal. Sometimes, newly rich people will not be socially recognized by the old upper class. Marriage with an old upper-class family is one way for a family in the new group to be acknowledged.

When the 1.5 percent of families who make up the upper class are subtracted from the 13 percent of families who earn above $30,000, 11.5 percent of all families remain who can be called upper middle class. This group includes the 10.5 percent who earn between $30,000 and $50,000 and the 1 percent who earn above $50,000 but who are not part of the upper class. Members of the upper middle class are owners of somewhat smaller investment capital and businesses; professionals like doctors and lawyers; executives; consultants with special skills; and stars of art and sport. Except for entertainment personalities, they are probably in this class because their parents were in it or near it, as it takes substantial resources to enter the upper middle class.

Looking down the chart at the two groupings that include the most families, we see that 41.1 percent of families earn between $15,000 and $30,000 annually, while 36.6 percent earn between $5,000 and $15,000. Almost all families in these two large groupings earn more than the official poverty level of $6,191 for a nonfarm family of four, and are not, therefore, considered by the government to be poor. Although the dividing lines between classes get fuzzy at this level, we might categorize those earning more than $15,000 a year.(which is $1,000 below the median income level) as the middle class. In general, the middle class includes businesspeople in middle management; small shop-owners; professionals working with public agencies; teachers; and some well-paid craftspeople and workers.

The group that earns more than the poverty level but less than $15,000 can be referred to as the lower middle class or the working class. The working class is generally defined by the type of work family members perform more than by income level. One source includes, as working class, "all nonprofessional and nonmanagerial workers in the primary industries, manufactur-ing, and the clerical and service sectors; nonadministrative state employees (who are mainly clerical and maintenance workers); as well as unwaged family members supported by such work-ers."[10] Since the workers mentioned above usually earn less money than workers in what are considered to be middle-class jobs, it is possible *roughly* to define working class in terms of income level.

Members of the working class are more likely than members of the middle class to be unemployed from time to time, and are therefore more likely to fall into poverty. There are not now and never have been enough jobs to go around, which is another way of saying that the United States never has full employment. The rates of unemployment vary depending on the state of the economy. In recessions, more people lose their jobs. In the depths of the Depression of 1929–1939, up to one-fourth of the working population was unemployed. The real rate of unemploy-ment is difficult to determine for any given time, because after many unsuccessful tries, some people give up looking for work and are no longer recorded as unemployed. They may go back to school and count as students, or, if they are female, they may now get counted as housewives. Some will have to go on welfare. Eighty percent of welfare recipients are children and their mothers, living on about two dollars a day per person, after the rent is paid. This is barely enough for food, much less for clothing, transportation, or anything else.[11] Most working-class families move through these situations at one time or another, living on some combination of wages, unemployment insurance,

Social Security, welfare, and food stamps. Working-class women are especially likely to fall into poverty when they are divorced or widowed, since women are paid, on the average, only 60 percent of what men are paid. A striking proportion of people in households with no adult men present live below the poverty level. In 1977, 32.8 percent of people in female-headed families or single-female households lived below the poverty level, as compared to 6.9 percent of people in families or households with adult males present.[12]

What is poverty? This is perhaps the cruelest distinction of all, because the figures are all so far below median income. Some social scientists suggest that the poverty level be defined as half the median income, which would be about $8,000. However, the government does not define families with incomes at half the median level as poor; it draws the poverty line lower still, at $6,191 for a nonfarm family of four. Nevertheless, even the government's low poverty level takes in over 10 percent of American families—and 11.6 percent of the American population. It includes approximately 25 million people—10 million of them children.[13] The overall *percentage* of people living under the poverty level is nearly the same as it was in 1900. Little has changed in income distribution since the beginning of this century.

In studying income distribution, one important guideline is the notion of median income. This is an imaginary line drawn through the middle of the wage-earning population, indicating that half of it earns more and half earns less than the specified figure. In 1977, the median income for all families—of all sizes, races, and ages—was $16,009.[14] Median income is also figured for different groupings of families—by race, number of wage earners, number of people in the family, etc. In 1977, the median income for all white families was $16,740; for all black families, it was $9,563; and for all black and other nonwhite families, it was $10,142. Families with one wage earner had a significantly lower median income in 1977 than families with two wage earners: $13,148 compared to $18,704.[15]

The U.S. Department of Labor has identified 1977 "standards of living" for an urban family of four that fall into three "budgets":

a higher budget level of at least $25,202; an intermediate budget
level of at least $17,106; and a lower budget level of at least
$10,481.[16] This lower budget level is considered by the govern-
ment to be a minimum standard of "comfort." Yet, as we saw,
many who earn below $10,481 are not considered poor. If we
include all those people who have family incomes below the
"lower budget" level, we see that between one-quarter and one-
third of the population of the United States lives below the
minimum standard of comfort as defined by the U.S. Government. The Department of Labor outlines how a family in each of
the "budget levels" might spend its annual income. Taking those
figures and interpreting them based on methods used by
Kenneth Keniston and the Carnegie Council on Children in
their book, *All Our Children: The American Family Under
Pressure*, the charts on pages 59–61 indicate what different
family incomes mean in terms of daily life.[17]

In fact, many families have to spend more than the charts allot
for certain categories—such as housing and food—in order to
survive. They will thus have even less money for other items,
including medical care and clothing. This is increasingly true as
a high rate of inflation means rapid price increases in virtually
every area of the economy. Most families in the United States
have little cushion for emergencies, much less for luxuries, and
are likely to fall into debt. Many families are either in poverty or
at its very edge, falling in and coming out again depending
on circumstance.

Taking a close look at the percentage of families in different
income groups, and considering what different incomes mean in
terms of ability to provide goods and services for a family,
graphically illustrates the vast differences among families in our
society. While 63.4 percent of families earn less than $20,000
annually, one upper-class family recently spent $20,000 in one
year on the family dog.[18] Although definitions of social class may
appear somewhat static, they show how belonging to a family of
a particular class helps determine how one grows up. The child
of two successful lawyers and the child of a janitor and a waitress
will have different real opportunities and different feelings
(text continued on page 62)

1977 LOWER BUDGET:
FOR A FAMILY OF FOUR
WITH AN INCOME OF $10,481

Category	Annual Cost	Interpretation
Food	$ 3,190	$61 per week or 73¢ per meal per person
Housing	$ 2,083	$173 per month for rent or mortgage, utilities, home furnishings, and maintenance
Transportation	$ 804	$67 per month for car payments, gas, oil, and repairs, or 55¢ per day per person for public transportation
Clothing and personal care	$ 1,110	$23 per month per person for shoes, clothing, cleaning, laundry, repairs, haircuts, soap, shampoo, toothpaste, etc.
Medical care	$ 980	$82 per month for health insurance, prescriptions, dental care, and uninsured portions of medical costs
Family consumption	$ 489	$2.35 per week per person for all leisure activities: vacations, entertainment, books, newspapers, etc.
Other costs	$ 472	$39 per month for gifts, contributions, life insurance, business-related and miscellaneous expenses
Compulsory Social Security and disability insurance	$ 632	6 percent of total income
Personal income tax	$ 720	6.9 percent of total income
Total	$10,481	

1977 INTERMEDIATE BUDGET: FOR A FAMILY OF FOUR WITH AN INCOME OF $17,106

Category	Annual Cost	Interpretation
Food	$ 4,098	$78 per week or 93¢ per meal per person
Housing	$ 4,016	$335 per month for rent or mortgage, utilities, home furnishings, and maintenance
Transportation	$ 1,472	$123 per month for car payments, gas, oil, and repairs, or $1.01 per day per person for public transportation
Clothing and personal care	$ 1,559	$32 per month per person for shoes, clothing, cleaning, laundry, repairs, haircuts, soap, shampoo, toothpaste, etc.
Medical care	$ 985	$82 per month for health insurance, prescriptions, dental care, and uninsured portions of medical costs
Family consumption	$ 909	$4.37 per week per person for all leisure activities: vacations, entertainment, books, newspapers, etc.
Other costs	$ 763	$64 per month for gifts, contributions, life insurance, business-related and miscellaneous expenses
Compulsory Social Security and disability insurance	$ 961	5.6 percent of total income
Personal income tax	$ 2,342	13.7 percent of total income
Total	$17,106	

1977 HIGHER BUDGET:
FOR A FAMILY OF FOUR
WITH AN INCOME OF $25,202

Category	Annual Cost	Interpretation
Food	$ 5,159	$99 per week or $1.18 per meal per person
Housing	$ 6,085	$507 per month for rent or mortgage, utilities, home furnishings, and maintenance
Transportation	$ 1,913	$159 per month for car payments, gas, oil, and repairs, or $1.31 per day per person for public transportation
Clothing and personal care	$ 2,265	$47 per month per person for shoes, clothing, cleaning, laundry, repairs, haircuts, soap, shampoo, toothpaste, etc.
Medical care	$ 1,027	$85 per month for health insurance, prescriptions, dental care, and uninsured portions of medical costs
Family consumption	$ 1,499	$7.21 per week per person for all leisure activities: vacations, entertainment, books, newspapers, etc.
Other costs	$ 1,288	$107 per month for gifts, contributions, life insurance, business-related and miscellaneous expenses
Compulsory Social Security and disability insurance	$ 985	3.9 percent of total income
Personal income tax	$ 4,980	19.8 percent of total income
Total	$25,202	

about their future as adults. One will probably have much more control over her or his life than the other, and with it is likely to come a sense of powerfulness and self-esteem. The two will grow up to be very different, no matter how equal they were in ability at the start. While social class is not a prison, it is a "track" that is hard to break out of without changing the rules of the game entirely. As things are now, it helps to be on the "inside track."

Who Is at Home? A person's first family experience is of the one into which he or she is born: the family of origin or "root" family. How many others are born into it, how the parents act in the home, and what other relatives live there will make an important difference, materially and psychologically. Social scientists who study hundreds of families are able to trace out broad patterns of behavior shared by families. While nobody likes to feel part of a statistic, and while there are many exceptions to the generalizations made, statistics do tell some important facts.

Perhaps the hardest fact to accept is that the kind of person we become is influenced by some factors beyond our control. Most people are willing to accept biological determinism, that is, the influence of physical heredity on who we are. Few, however, are willing to accept social determinism, that is, the influence of social heredity, such as class. Yet social class affects the size and structure of households and the behavior of families in them. One cannot cut oneself off completely from one's history.

Both household and family size and structure have changed a great deal among all groups since the beginning of this century. Most people born in the 1980s will have one sibling, two parents working outside the home, and no other relative living in their household. This is a significant change from the early twentieth century when households included many children, grandparents, and perhaps an aunt or uncle and a tenant or two. Some observers consider the change as a crisis in family life and in population replacement. But is it? Others have argued the opposite: that family planning for fewer children and the addition of a wife's outside income raises the family standard of living, or at least keeps it from falling down.

It is a fact that the national birthrate has been dropping

steadily, especially in the last twenty years. In the United States, fertility rates have fallen well below replacement level, down to an average of 1.8 children per woman over her lifetime.[19] This same trend exists in most advanced industrial nations. However, the lower birthrate does not mean that fewer women are having babies. In fact, a higher percentage of women than before are having babies, but each mother is having fewer. Today, the average woman spends far fewer years of her life bearing and raising children than women of the past. She has much more time left for other activities, including work outside the home. This trend has altered a woman's relation to the family. She is no longer the anchor for others who go "out" into the world. As long as women were seen as being the *core* of the family, rather than simply *part* of it, they did not have the freedom to go "out" in the same way. Now, their work outside the home is often indispensable for the family's well-being. Paradoxically, it may even have a good effect on children. Studies have shown that women working outside the home spend about the same amount of time *actively* involved with their children as do full-time housewives. They show that the quality of time spent with children, when it is planned into an employed woman's life, is often excellent.[20]

Going back to numbers: it would be a mistake to imagine this national average of 1.8 children per family to be a single new "norm" for all. The reality is that while all families are smaller than they used to be, the very poor and the very rich have somewhat more children than average. Some religious, racial, and ethnic groups, such as Catholics, blacks, Native Americans, and Hispanics, tend to have more children than other groups, such as Jews or white Protestants. And groups that tend to have large families have fewer children when they move up in social class, concentrating all resources on helping just a few individuals move up still further.

The upper class, like the aristocracy of old, maintains itself through large families which intermarry with other large families, thus concentrating and increasing their wealth. For this group, children are an asset for making alliances. Recently, however, even this group's members have been following closer to the national average for lower rates of childbirth.

At the other end of the scale, very poor people also have many children. At first glance, children don't seem to be an asset to a poor family. Yet they may be. Death rates are higher among the poor, especially in infancy and early childhood. So having three or four children may be a kind of guarantee that one or two will be alive when the parents are old. Also, many poor families are still close to their roots in another culture where larger families are the norm and are highly valued.

Among the urban poor, and especially among unmarried teenage women, children come earlier and more often than among more financially secure groups. A major reason is the lack of easily available contraceptive information and devices. Another may be that motherhood has some prestige as a sign of adulthood. Still another may be simply love of children and the satisfaction that comes from having them, especially when there may be few other opportunities for love and happiness. Finally, with a supportive network of family and friends, having a baby outside of marriage is less of a problem than it might be in other circumstances.

But numbers of children alone do not determine the size and shape of families. There is also the question of the presence and absence of other adults in the household and the relationships family members have with one another even when they live in different households. National averages reveal a great rise in the percentage of single and divorced women maintaining a household with only their children, but a drop in the comparative percentage of families headed by men alone.[21] Today, over 80 percent of single-parent families are woman-headed, whereas in 1940 only about 66.7 percent were. Part of this change reflects the fact that more single-parent families today are the result of divorce rather than of death of one parent. In divorce cases, most courts award custody of children to mothers. The statistics also reflect the rising number of children born outside of marriage in the first place. The increased ability of women to support themselves and their children is one factor allowing women more frequently to withdraw from undesirable marriages or to avoid them from the start. And the increase in social welfare services has also helped to make that possible. It is true, too, that conditions for receiving welfare aid often make it harder for a marriage to hold together. In any case, far more children today than ever before grow up with their mothers as the only major adult in the household for at least part of their lives.

Another change in the composition of households has been the disappearance of relatives such as grandparents, grown-up brothers and sisters, aunts, uncles, and cousins from the household. These members of the "extended family" (as distinct from the "nuclear family" of parents and children) are now more likely to be living apart. This means that a child growing up today will have intimate family relationships with very few people other than his or her parents and will see fewer relatives on a daily basis than in the early twentieth century. Those relatives may be visited regularly, however, and can remain important to children and adults.

In the mansions of the upper class, a child will encounter not only the nuclear family, but a stream of visiting uncles and aunts, first, second, and third cousins—perhaps staying for long periods of time. Kin are important to a class that defines itself mainly through its long line and significant ancestors. "The family" is for them not only its current members, but a name to be upheld. This is a point of pride, but may also be a burden. A young woman of the Rockefeller family once complained: "Within the family, one hardly ever talks directly about who we are without our Rockefeller identity, our social identity, very little about love or hate or anger, without all these other... attachments. It's really tragic. I think that's one of the sadder things about our family."[22]

Since all descendants share an economic and social legacy, they are likely to keep in close touch even with very distant relatives, including those who have married "out" and now carry different names. A family tree, or genealogy, for such a family can become enormous. A 1950 reunion of the Du Pont family, one of the oldest upper-class families in the United States, drew six hundred people. The full number of Du Pont descendants is close to a thousand.[23] One observer noted that family talk makes up much of the conversation of the upper class. They talk about who is related to whom more than about what anyone has achieved, since as a class they have already achieved what the majority aspires to.[24]

An upper-class child will also have servants to relate to, some of them very closely, like a nanny. Growing up with servants has been reported by those who have had them as both a blessing and a curse. Maids, cooks, chauffeurs, gardeners, and janitors can make one feel important, and can provide friendship and help. Sometimes they become substitute parents, if the father is away a lot and the mother is also busy. But usually parents discourage very close child-servant relationships, warning "not to get too friendly with the people who work for us."[25] These same children will be giving orders themselves some day and must learn to keep their distance. One girl explained how she was taught this lesson.

There came a day when my mother took me aside and she said I had to understand a few things. She told me that I was getting too old to play with the colored kids, and too old to be hanging around the kitchen and wasting my time.... I should be more polite with the maid and the cook, and say please—but when I want something, *ask*, and expect to get it! My mother showed me how she does it. I pretended to be the cook, and she talked to me.[26]

Such children have, in a sense, two families, their biological one and a larger one of "staff."[27]

Among the poor, patterns of large households appear for very different reasons. Here children may have a variety of adults caring for them because of need. For example, if the child's biological father cannot find a job, the mother may live with her own mother and other relatives or friends, all of them pooling their wages and other income, perhaps welfare, until things get better. (Most mothers who accept welfare aid go to work within four years of their child's birth, and one-third go back within the first year and a half.[28]) Poor people use their kin to help care for their children.

Living under the same roof is only one form of such sharing. Other pooling—of money, of clothes, of food—also occurs.[29] Children raised in such families often develop a sense of group and of sharing, rather than a narrower focus on self and on individual advancement. What may look like lack of ambition to an outsider is often group loyalty. No doubt, some may resent feeling held back. But in the long run, all one's kin together form a safety net against daily hardship and occasional .disaster. Cutting ties would be dangerous. And there is real love and caring, too, though it may have its price. The upper class has a similar sense of group primacy over the individual, but its reasons are different. They are to consolidate wealth, hold on to power, and keep others out.

The attitudes fostered in the uppermost and lowermost classes are in contrast to those in the broad middle, whose goal is often to rise higher on the social ladder. In the middle class and the upper segments of the working class, sheer survival is somewhat more secure than in poorer families. There is enough of a base from which to push upward as well as the desire to reach the top. Higher education is one way to move up. In 1979, college-bound high school seniors reported a median family income of $20,800. This is about $3,000 more than the national median income of white families and $9,000 more than that of nonwhite families.[30] Obviously, working-class families often cannot afford to send any children to college. Even in the middle class, families may have to make hard choices and not spend money on "less promising" members.[31]

The homes of people trying to realize the "American dream" of success are generally organized to meet that goal. Income earners will sacrifice some goods and pleasures for the future, but also will try to keep up appearances. A small nuclear family helps concentrate resources. A child growing up in such a home will have daily contact with parents and siblings, but will only see grandparents from time to time, and uncles, aunts, and cousins even less often, perhaps only on important holidays. Indeed, the "extended family" may even live in another city or town, since this aspiring group tends to move in search of better jobs or neighborhoods. One way in which the family may help a child to succeed is for the mother to go to work and earn additional money for college. Another way is for grandparents to help out. In the middle class and the upper segments of the working class, parents and their parents attempt to boost the most promising members of the next generation, but expect more distant relatives, like cousins, not to ask for help for their careers. The nuclear family becomes a small, sharp flying wedge for success.

This does not mean that upwardly mobile families always succeed. Recessions can push a family into unemployment and onto welfare aid. There are barriers to entry into the higher-paid professions. And the occasional disaster, such as an illness, can drain all the family's reserve of money and energy. The point is, in the middle class and the upper segments of the working class, hope is a dominant value motivating many people and helping to produce the small household of the current "norm" family.

In sum, the shapes of families differ a great deal by class. People of the uppermost and lowermost classes relate to more family members than do those in the broad middle class. In that sense, it could be said their families remain more extended than those in the middle, whose patterns produce the "norm." Of course, the lines between these classes are not rigid, and people do move up or down. When they do, they gradually change their attitudes and family shapes. When groups of the most diverse racial, religious, and ethnic backgrounds move up toward the median income level on the strength of fairly secure, prestigious, and promising jobs, they come to look more like one another than like their ancestors and relatives.[32] Most change their values slowly but surely, and shape their children to be quite different from themselves.

Roots

The family usually cares for its members and vice versa. Here is where one has the first experience of love, and of hate; of giving, and of denying; of ecstasy, and of deep sadness. Family is the place of greatest intimacy, physical and psychological; it is where people touch. Here the first hopes are raised and met—or disappointed. Here is where one learns whom to trust and whom to fear. Above all, family is where people get their start in life, where they retreat from the pressures of work and school, where they fall back in deepest need, and where they experience the most sharing, usually as a matter of course. Family is a group that eats together, sleeps together, plays together, and combines forces to survive together. Even when a family is not as "together" as a picture in a family album, its members *expect* at least some level of intimacy.

The emotional experience of family is often so intense that the people involved may not see their own patterns of behavior, more noticeable to outside observers. Strong feelings and passionate caring cannot only mask a clearer view, but can positively prevent it. People often tend to think that analysis takes the life out of a subject. Few individuals like to believe that their "natural" impulses have a kind of plan to them; they don't *feel* that "cold-blooded." And yet, studies by social scientists show just such patterns of behavior, as if there were a kind of overall will at work, conscious or not. This will is formed by the values of our culture and is therefore widely shared and rarely questioned; it is taken for granted and is considered natural rather than socially formed.

Many people hope to do more than just survive, they hope to "do well." This may mean different things to different people, but includes such general aims as good health; a pleasant home; a loving family and friends; a job that pays well and gives one a sense of accomplishment; independence or control over one's life; and leisure time. Probably the majority still dream the "American dream" of success, the hope that each generation will "do better" than the previous one. At the very least, each generation hopes the next will not "do worse." Downward mobility is uncomfortable and sometimes dangerous to survival. It is also often taken as personal failure, even when the circumstances may be beyond the person's control, as in times of major economic depression. Individuals trace upward and downward mobility in their lifetime, but so do families over generations. Families teach individuals the strategy they think will work for success. This process is part of the larger task of initiating children into society, and is called socialization.

Socialization, as the term implies, has to do with preparing a person to participate effectively in society. People are socialized differently if they are male or female and they are socialized differently depending on their family income and social status. In the United States, people are taught that all human beings are equal in potential. But since the United States is a society that ranks its members, most Americans are taught also to be unequal. This is a contradiction people live with. Of course, insofar as individuals all participate in the same culture, there is some shared socialization. But here the focus will be on the differences, which often get neglected in discussions of *the* family.

The family is the first, but by no means the only, institution that socializes young people. Others include school; religious bodies; cultural media such as television, books, newspapers, movies, songs; summer camp; Boy Scouts and Girl Scouts. The whole society socializes its young into its culture. In fact, more and more groups outside the family, including professionals who advise parents, have an important shaping effect. This can lead to some confusion, especially if there are mixed messages among socializers, such as "buy" and "save," "assert yourself" and "don't be different." Contradictory messages are built into the society's system of values, but they are first delivered by and practiced in the family.

Problems arise when families try to teach appropriate behavior in a context where what is appropriate may be changing. For example, rugged individualism is one value out of the American past, but acting like a cowboy in an office would not lead to a successful career. Paperwork and teamwork have replaced the individual physical derring-do of the Old West. Families prepare boys and girls for their futures partly by teaching them attitudes they consider appropriate for their sex. Today, this is more complicated, as ideas about what is "masculine" and "feminine" are changing. While women are still expected to be mothers and wives who take care of their families, most of them will also work for pay. Each of these activities requires somewhat different attitudes, a different balance of cooperation, competition, and self-assertion. Similarly, more and more young men will be caring for and playing with their children. This, too, requires traits different from those needed on the job. People are not simply born with such responses; they must learn them. The kind of adult one becomes has a lot to do with one's roots or family of origin.

How do families socialize children? By word and deed. The words are important not only for what they say, but for who says them and how, and for whether or not they contradict the deed. Most children are taught to respect their parents and other adults, for example. But children taught by servants whom their parents can discharge will probably have a different idea of their own power over others than will those taught by civil servants—like public school teachers, health officers, or social workers—who act superior to their parents. A young man from a rich family told this story.

My father had sent me to this third-rate prep school in Worcester, and told them that if they could keep me a year he'd buy them a swimming pool. When I learned about it, I bribed the chauffeur to come up and get me, and when he arrived, I walked into the headmaster's office, lit up a cigarette, told him, "You ain't gettin' no swimmin' pool," and walked out.[33]

Even though this young man was a rebel, he knew his own power even over his school. Compare this story with that of the youngsters whose mother, on welfare, was summoned to the school when they misbehaved:

The principal said that if Mrs. Santana found her children uncontrollable, she could take them to Family Court and have them declared PINS—Persons In Need of Supervision. He pointed out that this had the disadvantage of giving them a record with the court, and that the court could decide to remove them to a foster home. . . . He asked Mrs. Santana if she would be willing to take them to a doctor to be examined, and told her that the doctor might prescribe tranquilizers for them, which might quiet them down.[34]

Mrs. Santana was also told by caseworkers how to keep her house and whether or not to stay with her alcoholic husband. For Mrs. Santana's children, rebellion is a serious danger and they will know that adults of their class have little control, if any, over their school and over other authorities.

Behavior is also taught by reward and punishment. Since different families have different kinds and amounts of rewards to give, the ratio of reward to punishment will vary by class. Where there is little to give, material rewards may not be a major way of reinforcing good behavior. Behavior is also taught by example and by nonverbal signals, such as hugging, turning away, looking glad or grim, or not paying attention at all. These responses are often not calculated to teach behavior, but they serve that function nonetheless. And they can be influenced by factors outside the family, such as the way a parent feels about her or his work. For the homemaker, lawyer, bus driver, or factory worker, a bad day at work, too much overtime, or general unhappiness about one's job can influence the way one responds to one's children.

These are very general points about socialization. What is the actual experience of family for its very young members? Looking at class differences, two qualifications are important to remember: the amount of information available about each class is unequal, and each individual, each researcher, makes judgments that affect the way she or he understands and presents information. Least is known about the upper class, because its wealth and privilege protect privacy and keep out prying investigators. The very poor cannot protect themselves from intrusion, as has been noted. The upper middle and middle class, by contrast, often welcome information-seekers. Members of these classes take pride in their achievements and hope to use new information to further advantage. Investigators usually come from these groups, who can thus feel friends are studying them and will present them in a favorable light. In addition, there are many shared and overlapping characteristics between classes. Not surprisingly, this is especially true near the "dividing lines" of the classes. So, for example, the upper segments of the working class may look very much like parts of the middle class, while the lower segments of the working class may share certain characteristics with the poor. And there are exceptions to the rule in each class. Socialization is not a cookie mold, turning out identical individuals.

Reaching for the "American Dream." For many in the middle class and the upper segments of the working class, a major aim of socialization is to help their children realize the

"American dream." Within these groups, a lot of energy goes into trying to move up and avoid falling down. This means developing personal ambition, a deeply felt need to achieve success, and the self-discipline and independence necessary for such achievement. It also means knowing when to compete and when to cooperate, when to be tough with others and when to please others. These contradictory traits—being individualistic sometimes and conforming sometimes—look like opportunism to critics. Flexibility is hypocrisy to some, but a virtue to others. It means being able to recognize new opportunities and act on them, to change manners and customs to fit new social settings. An example of this is the executive of Italian parentage who changed his eating habits several times in his life. As he "made it" up the social ladder, he switched from pasta and red wine to beef, beer, and beans; later to steak, seafood, and Scotch. Not until he was fully accepted by his local elite did he begin serving dinners of "authentic" ethnic food such as pizza and red wine.[35] Behind this story of dining habits lies another one of human relationships. This man had to be willing to leave old friends behind and to make new ones.

Upwardly mobile people trying to get to higher levels are more open than people of the upper class who, by and large, stay "exclusive," that is, limited to each other. Moving up the class hierarchy means getting past barriers put there just to keep strangers out, and then being willing to make friends with the people who tried to keep one out in the first place. Such changes are difficult. What does one do with old friends who don't "fit in" with new ones, who talk, dress, and eat "wrong" and go bowling instead of sailing? They may have to be dropped. Some may be kept out of loyalty or affection or as a "fallback" in case success doesn't last. For males, such choices usually come up around career advancement; for females, they are more often related to marriage prospects, though more women now are also choosing careers. Meeting "better people" is considered a desirable goal, and children of the upwardly mobile are trained to do that.

Flexibility in relationships requires openness, trust, and willingness to take risks, including that of rejection. So aspiring middle-class families try to raise "well-adjusted" children who have enough trust to cope with changing situations but also

enough mistrust to avoid "bad influences" and to look out for
competitors. It is a delicate balance not easily achieved or always
held. The family itself carries mixed messages. On the one hand,
family is supposed to be—and often is—a safe place, where
people may express themselves freely; cry, jump for joy, act
babyish even if they're middle-aged, daydream aloud, be a little
crazy. Behavior that would cause one to be expelled from any
other group is tolerated within the family, and this toleration
breeds trust. But there is another side, which sometimes takes
over: competition for nurturance and for goods—not only
between siblings, but also between mother and father and
parents and children—and murderous rage. Recent reports show
a shocking amount of physical and mental abuse, even murder,
especially of children and women, in families of all classes.[36]

The upwardly mobile family teaches the contradictions of
openness versus holding back and holding on, of sharing versus
competing, by the way it actually works, as well as by what it
says. Young people are taught to do better than their parents, but
sometimes they are resented when they succeed. Parents may
say, "I want my kids to be better off than I was." But they may also
wonder, "Who do they think they are? Spoiled rotten and they
think they know everything better." Upward mobility usually
takes some sacrifice, made in love but also with bitterness.
Success is the goal, but with it can come greater distance
between parents and children. Often a whole family feels
anxious about success and failure.

What methods do families use to teach their children behavior
that will help them move up the social and economic ladder?
Denying or offering love or money are two major ones. Parents,
especially mothers, who are generally assigned the main tasks of
early socialization, will give a hug and a kiss for good behavior
and be cold and disapproving or administer a slap for bad
behavior. In the nuclear family household, where children are
isolated from adults other than their parents, the giving or
withholding of parental love is a very powerful force. The effect
is to create feelings of shame and guilt for wrongdoing and
feelings of being unworthy of love. Later on, as an adult, the
person may recreate these feelings that were learned as a child

and regulate her or his own behavior. Another mechanism for socialization is material reward or penalty. Examples of this include getting a camera for a good report card or losing one's allowance for coming home late. Obviously, families with extra money for rewards can use this means most effectively.

Reasoning or persuading is also an important form of socialization in many middle-class families. When a parent engages in discussion about *why* it is in a child's best interest not to annoy the neighbors, the child is being trained to think and verbalize. This is useful preparation for school and for the young adult's own later attempts to influence others. On the other hand, such "reasonableness" may cover a parent's strong emotion, such as anger, and may be experienced by children as insincerity. What is being learned here is impulse control. For those with big hopes for the future, impulse control is especially important. For example, fighting is discouraged; in another class and neighborhood, fighting may be unavoidable and even absolutely essential for survival. Among the upwardly mobile, impulsive generosity, like giving away toys to friends, may be discouraged. Elsewhere, it may establish a pattern of give-and-take for essential items like food. Expression of sexual feelings is also likely to be held back more among the ambitious, since it might lead to early parenthood or marriage, which could keep young people from putting energy and money into a career and from making a careful choice of marriage partner.

Finally, special lessions in the social graces, such as music or sports, and social contacts through carefully planned parties or outings are part of the grooming of middle-class children. This is done so they will be comfortable with the "right people." Parents of this aspiring group, more than most others, will look for guidance from professionals and will read books on child rearing, like Dr. Spock's *Baby and Child Care*. They want to know the latest scientific information on how best to create an adult likely to succeed in the society. However, since experts' opinions change rapidly—for example, as to whether children should be raised strictly or permissively—even science gives an anxious parent no guarantees.

(text continued on page 78)

Today's Varied Families

In the United States in the 1980s, it is difficult, if not impossible, to define the "typical" family. Families may consist of mother, father, and children; of stepparents and stepchildren; of one parent and her or his children; of two unrelated people with or without children. And, a growing number of families are made up of two middle-aged or older people whose children are grown and living in other households. Families vary in other ways too: in regard to their income and thus their ability to provide material goods; in how they relate to kin who do not live within the household.

Left: a Chicano couple. Top right: a mother and three children. Bottom right: mother, father, and child.

Getting By. In some working-class families, especially those with incomes close to the median level of $16,009, children are socialized to be upwardly mobile in much the same way that middle-class children are. Whether this happens depends, to a large degree, on the kinds of jobs that the employed family members hold. If someone in the family has a relatively secure, high-paying, unionized job, his or her family may have the resources and hope necessary to help the children move up the social ladder. As family income moves farther away from the median, however, this is more and more difficult to do. Many working-class families must concentrate on surviving. Moving up may be only a faint hope, if even that. In one study of working-class families with a median income of $12,300, the overwhelming fact of life for the families was their nearness to poverty.[37] When this is the case, children will be socialized differently than when the hope of upward mobility is a dominant value.

As a realistic response to their past and present experiences, many working-class families convey to their children the idea that long-range planning is pointless. Working-class people generally look for decent-paying jobs early in life and have fewer hopes of going to college than their middle-class counterparts.[38] Because verbalization will be less important in the jobs that children of the working class will be employed in, socialization is done less through persuasion than through direct means like hugging or hitting.

Those living in official poverty obviously have even fewer choices and fewer chances to move up in the class hierarchy, and this undoubtedly affects the way they raise their children. There are rarely enough resources to help children find the time, quiet place, or peace of mind to study for a career. As success in our society is so largely figured in terms of money, people who do not measure up in this way may feel like failures and lose their self-respect. For example, fathers who cannot meet the needs of their families on substandard wages sometimes leave their families altogether rather than face their failure as "head of the family." Others may continue to contribute money whenever they can, but may not participate much in family life and instead spend time in a bar or on the street corner.[39] This does not mean they don't love their wives and children. It only means that lack of self-esteem is one of the "hidden injuries of class" that make it harder for families to hold together in poverty than in affluence.[40]

The exclusive clubs and institutions of the wealthier strata of society keep poor people out and, in doing so, keep them from meeting others who could help them to improve their situation. This, too, adds to feelings of hopelessness which dampen ambition. A major danger of poverty is the vicious cycle of need, insecurity, and low self-esteem. It could go round and round for several generations in a family, or only last part of one lifetime. Most of the jobs that poor people hold—sweeping or loading, waiting on tables, cleaning offices or homes, picking fruit and vegetables—offer few routes to upward mobility. In some poor families, among migrant workers for example, children are employed at a very young age, and work then becomes part of their socialization experience.

The lives of poor children are not as private or as limited to contact with a nuclear family as are those of upper middle-, middle-, and working-class children. Their homes may be so small and crowded that they cannot stay in them very long and may spend more time in public places like the street. They also may experience control by outside agencies, such as welfare and charitable organizations. People from these agencies observe their life-style and try to advise them on how to live. And the physical homes themselves change often as mortgages foreclose, evictions occur, and urban renewal forces residents to move.

Out of necessity and to protect themselves from too much control, poor families tend to use self-help when possible. Therefore, a wide network of kin remains important. For example, a father may not be able to support his children all of the time, but his mother and some of his brothers and sisters can and do pitch in.[41] Or, if a family loses its home, some family members may live with a grandmother, an uncle, or an aunt. In such a case, the nuclear family may not be living together, yet it will remain a family, if not a household.

But the kind of help available is limited. Group needs and group loyalty may make it hard for individuals to deny help to their relatives and to hoard resources in order to move into a higher social class. One study of poor families, for example, explains what happened when one woman's uncle died and left her $1,500 from a small, run-down farm. It covered her niece's telephone bill, a trip for relatives to visit a sick uncle, travel expenses for relatives to attend the funeral of that uncle, the burial of a former boyfriend, a sister's overdue rent, school clothes for the woman's children and grandchildren, a winter coat for herself, and shoes for her husband. In a family with fewer emergencies to meet, the $1,500 might have gone to one person's college tuition or into the bank.[42] It would take luck and sometimes ruthlessness to move up from and out of some of these situations. A woman who became a famous author felt guilty all her life for leaving her poor family behind on a dirt farm.[43]

How do families respond to life in poverty? For one thing, uncertainty about the future makes long-range planning most difficult in this class. Children may be *told* to think ahead about what they will be when they grow up, but they may *see* that the unexpected is the rule of the day. For example, money is not always around, so the time to buy things is when it is available. A mother may buy a toy for her baby when her husband brings home a paycheck. She may know that the paycheck won't cover their expenses in any case, so she may not feel compelled to count her pennies. In a poor family, all members must pitch in and help. Children do some of the housework and help care for their sisters and brothers. They also earn money whenever they can, even if this cuts into schoolwork.

Outbursts of love and rage occur more freely in the poor family. Discipline is sometimes harsh, and children are expected to obey. There is less reliance on "how-to" books for child rearing. Both sexes are taught to be tough-minded, obedient, respectable, and also prepared to deal with living in hard times. On the other hand, forms of escape like drinking and drug abuse, which are kept better hidden among more affluent groups, spill out in public among the poor and provide opposite models for children. The same is true for sexual activity. Girls, especially, are raised with strict warnings against it. Yet sexuality is one of the few free pleasures to be had. As a result, the double standard, which allows men more sexual freedom than women, is often violated, though it remains important in theory. And while people of all classes get mixed messages about "proper" behavior, children of the poor seem to get the most mixed messages of all. Also, because there are less resources available, mistakes may be more serious for poor people and can have devastating long-term effects.

The Wealthy and Powerful. What about the minority at the top, the people who already have the worldly goods and status to which others aspire? How are their children raised? As noted earlier, the very rich are the hardest to study, because their wealth and power allow them to protect their privacy, except in a few sensational cases. However, some of their own members have told stories about their families, and reporters and biographers have caught glimpses of upper-class life, so we are not entirely in the dark. The picture that emerges is less glamorous and less lurid than that painted by popular magazines. In fact, it is a harsh picture, in some ways. Rules and regulations put family interest before that of individuals, because the family has a name to uphold and wealth and importance to maintain.

A child here is charged with carrying family wealth into the next generation. The family prepares the child for this role in various ways: mixing with children of other upper-class families is an important one. Organizing social life is considered women's special job, so girls learn it early. Parties are serious matters. For one thing, whom one invites makes a difference. If someone from a lower-class family ends up marrying into the upper class, she or he either contributes little or drains off wealth to her or his own family. Another member of the upper class, by contrast, can add wealth and prestige to a family. As one upper-class father told his daughter: "It's best to marry someone who's pretty much like yourself."[44] This is different from the message middle-class girls get from many movies, stories, and even their parents about marrying a "Prince Charming" to "better" herself. In fact, most of the marriages in the upper class are with one another. Flashy "out-marriages" that attract publicity are rare. Social columns in the newspapers tell the deeper truth.

How is a girl prepared for this sheltered but important social life? Partly by her family and partly by different kinds of hired socializers. Probably she will have a nurse or governess first, and then attend an exclusive kindergarten and private school. Wealthy black people have tended to send their children to their own exclusive and formal private schools, though some more racial integration may now be taking place.[45] In private schools, a girl is taught academic subjects, and will also take special classes in dancing, riding, and foreign languages. She will probably go to boarding school when she is in her teens. Until quite recently, these schools were more concerned with training their students to exercise the social power that would be theirs when they grew up than with educating them in academic subjects. Discipline was severe, on the grounds that "you cannot learn to give orders until you take them."[46] In the past, boarding school taught estate management: the order of servants in a great household; how the butler should answer the telephone; the proper place setting for a twelve-course dinner; and the difference between high and low tea and what to serve at each.[47] Today, things have changed somewhat, and many exclusive private schools provide a fine academic education and excellent preparation for college. However, the message upper-class girls get from their families has changed less. One girl who wanted to be a traveling reporter was told by her father that "no lady ought to do that kind of work," while her mother granted only that "it wouldn't be a bad life—for a year or two, before marriage." She was also discouraged from her next ambition, to become a doctor. Finally, she accepted that it was her business to learn to run a house and deal with servants.[48] Another daughter took an interest in her father's business, but was told there was room only for his son and nephews.[49] Although patriarchy cuts across class lines, there is more real power behind it at these uppermost levels of wealth.

The milestones in the life of an upper-class young woman have generally been not school graduations, but steps toward marriage. She is considered officially marriageable after her debut, a "coming-out" party that takes place around her nineteenth or twentieth birthday. This and marriage itself are the major events the family plans for, although this may be changing somewhat. One author tells the story of a young woman who went to college and was an "A" student hoping to graduate with honors, when her mother pulled her out of school in her junior year. The mother said: "Dear, you little sister is coming out in another year, and I can't afford both a wedding and a debut in the same year. Pick one of your beaus and we will arrange a wedding in June." Tearfully, the young woman complied, though she did not love any of the boys she knew then.[50] She was not the only one of the "generations of ladies who discover how life is sacrificed to serving the fortune."[51]

A boy of the upper class is also expected to make the family name and fortune his career, but in a different way. He will be expected to learn how to rule. It is no coincidence that schools like Groton graduate, in one class, "a secretary of the army, an assistant secretary of state, presidents of the First National City Bank, the Mellon Bank, and the Celanese Corporation, ambassadors to the Philippines and to Indonesia, a novelist, a Benedictine monk, some eminent lawyers and doctors, no failures—in a worldly sense."[52] Discipline is stiff, almost military, and some boys rebel to the point of being expelled from many schools until they submit. Even those who become more radical and think about democratizing society according to its highest ideals, usually outgrow that impulse.[53] Academic subjects, then, do matter for upper-class boys, and most of them proceed to college, especially to Ivy League schools like Harvard, Princeton, or Yale. Since they will inherit controlling shares of the economy, they generally concentrate on learning economics, law, and political science. They emerge as corporation lawyers, Wall Street investment bankers, or business executives. They are usually discouraged from going into "inappropriate" careers such as teaching, writing, or scientific study.[54]

Upper-class children are carefully socialized to fill their parents' shoes. What they need to *know* is important, but even more important is what they need to *feel*. One observer has called the upper-class feeling one of "entitlement."[55] It means having confidence about the future, expecting to get what one wants. Regardless of what they actually achieve, these individuals usually have a high opinion of themselves compared to less affluent people. This is true even if they fall short by their own standards.

Does this mean that children of this class are happier than most? There is no answer to such a question, because happiness is extremely difficult to measure and compare. Many have complained they felt unloved and not as close to their parents as they would have liked to be. Others have felt extremely close. Some have been afraid of not living up to a famous family name; others have felt secure in their heritage. Very few have turned their backs on it. Whatever they may feel, these children grow to hold considerable power. And their family life has socialized them for this role.

People of Color. For whites in the United States, a long ancestry brings prestige. It has generally been denied to Native American Indians who were here first. It has also been denied to black people, who were brought to the United States by force, and some of whom can trace their roots back for many generations. Discrimination has put up barriers against people of color and has made it harder for them to fulfill the "American dream."

Since the late nineteenth century, however, there has been a small group of very wealthy blacks in the United States. The older black elite owns landed properties and holds important posts in education and the professions. Among them are the descendants of Frederick Douglass, the famous abolitionist, and the Syphax family that traces its ancestry back to Robert E. Lee, the Civil War general from an upper-class white family. Other wealthy blacks have made their fortunes from recent successful business ventures, as in the case of John Johnson of the Johnson Publishing Company and George Johnson (no relative) who made his money in the cosmetics industry. Like the white upper class, the older black elite may look down on "new money" and accept newly rich families only slowly into its social circles and for marriage. People who come up from poverty suddenly and lack the socialization of the rich are generally not fully accepted as equals. One wealthy young woman found out she was related to Joe Louis, the former world champion of boxing. Her grandmother said: "I know, I'm sorry. I hoped you'd never know."[56]

Although wealthy black and Hispanic people in the United

States clearly have many privileges over less affluent
of their races, they too are subject to racism and discri
One Chicano father told his daughter that Anglos wo
him buy certain lands at any price, because they did not want
Mexican-Americans "in" on them.[57] Because children of the
wealthy may grow up in sheltered environments, they may be
somewhat surprised by the amount of prejudice they experience
when they enter the larger society.

For many people of color, however, discrimination is more
than a personal insult. It is a sentence of poverty. The majority of
poor people in the United States are white, because whites are
the majority of the population. However, a far larger *proportion*
of people of color are poor. Like everybody else, one way they
handle the problems of poverty is through family strategies.
Sometimes, these solutions have been given bad names by racist
interpreters. But the truth is that color has little to do with it; the
closer all people come to affluence, the more their families act
alike. Class, not race, is the strongest influence on family forms
and behavior.

Rather than examining the relationship of racial discrimination to poverty, some have tried to "explain" the higher percentage of black and hispanic people living in poverty by their family
structures. Black families have been called matriarchal (ruled by
the mother) and Chicano families have been called patriarchal
(ruled by the father). These supposedly opposite family structures and relationships have been blamed for the apparent
failure of many members of each group to rise to a high
socioeconomic level. In other words, black and Chicano families
have been blamed for the effect of racial discrimination. The
black matriarchy theory asserts that black mothers dominate
their sons and cause them to be less manly and therefore less
successful. The supposed solution, according to these arguments, is to reduce the power of the mother. The Chicano
patriarchy theory claims that Chicano fathers hold their children back by being tyrannical. The solution to Chicano poverty,
according to this theory, is supposed to be to reduce the power of
the father.

These arguments overlook racial and economic discrimination. They are also wrong for other reasons. One is that the black

family cannot be called matriarchal by any stretch of the imagination, since rule implies power. Black women in our society are economically and politically one of the weakest and most disadvantaged groups of all. They earn less money than men of all races and than white women, yet often carry great responsibility for their families. Given the odds against them, their struggle is heroic. Black median income is about 60 percent of white median income, or sixty cents to every dollar.[58] In the recession of 1974/75, unemployment and underemployment affected over one-quarter of the black labor force—about 3 million people.[59] In the inner cities, it was higher—about 50 percent. Black men were laid off at record pace, often following the "last hired, first fired" policy. Their jobs in construction and manufacturing were among the hardest hit. Black women and teenagers fared a little better, as their jobs were mostly in services, but large numbers of them also had to leave the labor market altogether. Many middle-income black families, who had reached that level because both parents worked for pay, lost at least one wage earner and fell back into poverty. In 1977, 37 percent of black families earned less than $7,000, as compared to 14.2 percent of white families,[60] and this despite the fact that people of color had more education than ever before. Approximately 29 percent of the nonwhite population lived below the poverty level in 1977, as compared to less than 9 percent of the white population.[61]

One of the effects of poverty on black families has been to increase the number of households headed by women. In the face of constant higher unemployment for black men than for white men, fatherhood has often been difficult. Though statistics are not completely reliable and do not tell when strategies are only temporary, it seems that now, more than one out of three of all black children live with only their mothers, whereas ten years ago one out of four did.[62] What is less often mentioned is the other side of that coin: the majority—two out of three—live with both parents. Obviously the mother plays a central role in the black family, but it is difficult to see how it is a destructive role.

Chicano families have been labeled with an opposite stereotype. They are considered father-dominated, with men laying great value on their ability to produce children and to exert authority in their households. *Machismo* is the Spanish term, meaning manliness, that describes these qualities. It is true that Mexican culture, which is Spanish-influenced, has given much power to the male. Ancient Roman law, which is the historical basis for Spanish law and which the conquerors imposed on Mexico, gave the father power over the life and death of his family. This had meaning for wealthy propertied families whose households included slaves. For poor Mexicans, however, reality was very different. Today, for those living in lands later conquered by North Americans, it is even more different. Mexican-American men with skills such as carpentry now do unskilled work such as fruit harvesting. It is frequently the only available employment. Women's wages, usually from work in the service trades or in the fields, have been an essential part of the family income. In the Chicano community, about one-third of the women raise their children alone or with kin. This pattern is similar to that in the black community, and is common among many poor white people too.[63] In addition, in Chicano culture, godparents take important responsibility for orphans or poor children. And even in families where both parents are present in the household, the mother may be the main disciplinarian of children. Over half the Chicano respondents in a recent survey said their mothers had more influence over them than their fathers.

It is true that many Chicano men still consider their wives' frequent pregnancies to be a sign of male sexual prowess. It is also true that most Chicano husbands control the family's purse strings. This is not so different from white families, except for the amount of money involved: Chicano median income is about 65 percent of the white median income, just a little bit higher than the black median income.[64]

By comparing Chicano and black families, we can see that evidence does not support the stereotypes, of "matriarchy" and "machismo." Mothers are central figures in most poor households of any color. It is cruel and racist to blame a group for developing skills to survive in a system marked by social inequality.

Sex Roles. In families of all classes and races, one of the most important kinds of socialization girls and boys receive is about gender—what it means to be a woman or a man. In the upper class, girls generally learn to rule the social sphere while boys learn to exercise political and economic power. In other classes, too, girls and boys are raised differently because they are expected to take on distinct masculine and feminine adult roles. Children may be pressured into conforming to "appropriate" sex-role behavior. A seven-year-old boy liked a girl of the same age who lived in his apartment building. The other boys teased him and beat him up when they saw him playing with her. The girl started to walk ten yards behind him on the way home from school, so the other boys wouldn't think he was going to play with her.[65]

In most families, fathers have more power than mothers, partly because they are the only or the largest money earner. "Patriarchy" is the term for fathers ruling the family. Fathers may rule kindly or unkindly under patriarchy; the point is that they expect obedience. Love may soften patriarchal power or even seem to reverse it, but it generally remains in the background. It takes on different forms in different kinds of families.

Men who work for a boss whom they must obey may sometimes feel the need to be powerful at home. A salesman testified: "All day, 'Yes sir,' 'Yes ma'am.' I don't mind it so bad, but when I get home I don't want more of it."[66] Another man said plainly: "I'm the guy who brings the bread home. So they *have* to have some respect for me. I respect them because they are my children, but I am their daddy, so they have to...they have to follow the rules I set at home."[67] But this freedom for the father may cost other family members theirs. Many women and children don't like feeling dominated and experience the father's control as oppressive.

From his father's behavior, a boy is likely to learn that patriarchal authority can be his some day. He will not have to be told; he will *feel* his "rights" and duties. He may come to believe that making a "good living" is important for his self-respect and for the respect and obedience of others. This is why failure may seem so threatening to males. It means not only poverty, but loss of control. If patriarchy is his model, it may be hard for a boy to imagine that self-respect need not come from control over others, but through egalitarian relationships. A girl may learn from a patriarchal family that she should be like her mother: someone who cares for the family's material needs like cooking, cleaning, and laundering, and who also gives comfort and psychological support. She may see her job as assisting others with their lives, rather than as building a life for herself.

In middle-class families, relations between husbands and wives, while not equal, still appear to be somewhat more equal than in other classes. Often, both middle-class parents work outside the home to keep up or raise the family's standard of living and to pay for their children's higher education. They may share some leisure-time pursuits, like visiting, playing cards, and traveling. They are likely to consult with one another about major decisions such as moving or buying a new car, although the husband's preference may carry more weight. Often, middle-class parents discuss how they will raise their children and agree on certain goals and methods. But generally it is left to the mother to work out these methods in practice. In middle-class families, the language of equality may mask or seem to contradict the reality of male authority. Because children see the mother "in charge" in the home, they may believe she dominates in ways. Yet they may see males dominating in other ways and may see—or hear about—males and females as equals in still other areas. They get mixed messages about sex roles. This may be one reason why most of the people who are intentionally trying new gender roles today come from the middle class. Many young women from this group are now choosing to have careers and delaying marriage and motherhood. And some people are stretching out beyond the nuclear family to new forms, like communal living.

Generally, there is more rigidity about proper male and female roles in working-class families. Although in many working-class families, both husband and wife work full-time outside the home, the wife is more likely than in the middle-class family to view her job as a temporary necessity rather than as a chosen career. Leisure activities are more likely to be sex-segregated in working-class families. And there is less of a language of equality between husband and wife than in middle-class families, although whether in fact there is less equality is difficult to determine.[68] Children's "inappropriate" sex-role behavior is less apt to be tolerated than it is in middle-class families. This may be partly because working-class families perceive that they can less afford to experiment with unknowns. With fewer resources, fewer options are available to children and families.

Branches

Like branches of a tree, new families grow out of old ones. The families people form as adults are strongly linked to their families of origin. Like everything else, the feeling of love, which often leads to marriage, does not exist in a vacuum. It is shaped by cultural forces, such as the law, social pressure, socialization.

The experience of growing up in a family sets patterns, which generally include a preference for continuing to live that way and also a tendency to recreate the satisfactions and problems of the original family. In 1976, 69 percent of people in the United States over the age of eighteen were married, though a large and growing minority—18 percent—were still single. Of the remainder, 8 percent were widowed and 5 percent divorced, and this 13 percent had not remarried at the time of the count. Furthermore, in 1976, about 90 percent of all people over the age of thirty had been married at least once. From these figures, one might conclude that younger people are just putting marriage off a little longer, but that it is still the predominant life-style in the United States.[69]

On the other hand, it is interesting to note new trends. More people than ever before are living together without being married—twice as many in 1978 as in 1970.[70] In 1978, there were 1.1 million such households in the United States, though they remained a small fraction of the 48 million traditional husband-wife households. Another striking trend is the increase in the number of people who live alone. In 1978, about 50 million Americans—representing 20 percent of all households—lived alone. And 8 million families in 1978 were designated as "female headed," compared to 5.6 million in 1970.[71]

Choosing to Marry. The majority of the population continues to try marriage. How do those who marry choose their partners? Falling in love may be a marvelous surprise for the individuals involved, but statistics show a less exciting, more predictable pattern. Dating is a social custom, the ultimate purpose of which is the selection of a mate for marriage. Selection means choice, and dating also puts limits on choice. Among some groups, such as Orthodox Jews, dating and marriage may be arranged by parents. For most Americans, dating appears to be quite free. However, limits are set by approval or disapproval of parents and friends; possible accepted places to meet; and notions of ideal qualities, which are learned from family, friends, school, and the media. There are other limitations, too: close relatives, people of the same sex, and people of different races are often discouraged from viewing each other as lovers. The law reinforces some of these customs. In about two-thirds of the states, first cousins may not marry. Another common prohibition forbids stepparents and stepchildren from marrying. Before a Supreme Court decision of 1967, twenty-nine states forbade certain types of interracial marriages. No states presently recognize marriage between people of the same sex. In fact, laws are being considered now that would make it hard for homosexuals even to live together, by depriving them of their civil rights.[72] A strong gay male and lesbian rights movement is currently fighting such violations of freedom.

Freedom to choose a mate is limited also by one's family of origin. The United States is far from the melting pot it was once thought to be. Most people marry within their own ethnic group, though religion also plays an important part. Thus, Catholics usually marry other Catholics and Jews, other Jews. Protestants, being by far the largest religious group (they make up more than half the population) have the smallest fear of losing their identity and so marry non-Protestants more freely.[73] The tendency to "marry one's own kind" is called homogamy. In 1968, homogamy in race was 99 percent; in religion, 90 percent; and in social class, 50 to 80 percent. The upper class and the very poor marry inside their group most; the middle groups have the least homogamy. Being neither at the top nor at the bottom of the social hierarchy, they are most likely to move up or down, and their marriage patterns reflect this movement.[74]

But homogamy, while still strong, is falling off. Sometimes there are trade-offs: an individual from a lower status group who has "succeeded" may marry an individual from a higher status group who has not achieved success. For example, a black or Jewish person who becomes an executive or diplomat might marry a white Protestant person from a "good" old family that has lost its wealth or standing.[75] In other words, someone moving up may meet someone moving down; a marriage between them can bring status to the upstart and new wealth to the holder of a "good" name. The very rich, however, rarely meet and marry outside of their class. The same is true for the very poor. Explicit and implicit membership rules and prohibitive costs in some social spaces keep the Cinderella story a fairy tale rather than a reality. Social background helps decide whether people go to a country club, a church dance, or a local disco. So dating occurs between preselected groups in limited areas. Whom one falls in love with, therefore, is not purely accidental.

"Love and marriage, love and marriage, go together like a horse and carriage." So goes the old song. But what is meant by "The honeymoon is over"? Most couples who have been happily married for a long time say that their relationship has changed over the years, from one kind of love to another. Although the intensity and excitement of a new relationship is difficult to maintain, it is often replaced by a different kind of closeness. One woman writes that what is important to her about her marriage of many years is "having someone close to you who knows you well enough to be accepting; who knows and shares your history, and thus is helpful about making choices; who is there when you are ill or unhappy or worried, as well as when you want to have fun, share sports and other leisure-time activities, discuss your work, etc."[76] This is the model one hopes for, the ideal at the end of the romantic movie: "And they lived happily ever after."

But there is another possible scenario, which also often occurs because, of course, the end of one movie is just the beginning of another, much longer one: life together. There are many symptoms that suggest that marriage is not always the blissful relationship of our dreams. One is the shocking amount of physical violence that occurs. One estimate is that 28 million women—almost half of all wives—have been beaten by their husbands at some time.[77] Violence can escalate in the whole family. Most murders occur in families or between "loved ones." Many, though not all, get reported to the police. Violence short of murder occurs more often. One young woman, accused of beating and neglecting her children, remembered her own childhood:

She saw herself at age five, sitting with her brother Johnnie at the kitchen table in their East St. Louis house. They were eating macaroni, she remembered, and Johnnie had thrown some at her. It began as fun, a game, but it had soiled a favorite dress, and she was angry.

She cried, but Johnnie only laughed. He looked at his parents, then threw more food at her. Marlene cried louder, and standing in her chair she leaned over the table to hit him. Her father yanked Johnnie out of his seat and without saying a word stood him on the floor and whacked him on the buttocks and the back of the legs. They boy cried out in pain. Her mother screamed that it was Marlene who had started the ruckus and went to punish her. Her father tried to stop his wife, but she reached out, resting her weight on the table, and slapped Marlene hard across the top of the head. The girl sobbed bitterly. Her father picked her up in one arm and tried to comfort her. With his free hand he slapped his wife across the face. Without waiting she hit him back, splitting his lips and scratching at his cheeks. He dropped Marlene, grabbed his wife by the wrists, then suddenly let go and punched her on the side of the head. Marlene and Johnnie heard the sound of the punch and saw blood flowing from their mother's eye and mouth.[78]

While this is not typical behavior, it is not all that unusual, either. Spouse and child battering has been recognized as a foremost national problem.

The rising divorce rate also raises questions about living "happily ever after." The divorce rate has been going up for the past fifteen years. It is estimated that nearly four of every ten existing marriages will end in divorce.[79] By 1978, one out of every five children was cared for by one parent.[80] On the other hand, many divorced people remarry, usually other divorced people. Most remarry within three years, though women remarry later than men and sometimes not at all. This is mainly because men can and do marry much younger women, while younger men are less available for older women.

Obviously there are contradictions here. People testify to the satisfactions of marriage and keep marrying and remarrying. Yet many people are unhappy within their marriages. What is going on?

When two people live together, many problems come up for them as individuals and as a couple. Money, sex, and children are some of the biggest. In examining these problems, it is helpful to look at how they relate to men's and women's unequal status in the family. Many laws keep women subordinate, especially after marriage. In some states, married women lose some of their rights to control property, and they cannot make contracts as they could when single or as men can before and after marriage. Some states allow a husband to control his wife's earnings and property and to dispose of them without her consent. They do not give a wife the right to a share of her husband's earnings besides what is necessary for running the household, even if she paid for the schooling he needed for a professional job. Many women, divorced by their husbands after a long life of service, have nothing to show for their work. Less than one-fourth of court-awarded alimony is ever paid.[81]

Law thus gives men an advantage in marriage. But the economy alone ensures it. Men have had a main say over the lives of the people who depend on them because they earn more and therefore control resources in the family.[82] Now this is changing somewhat. Half of the women in the United States work for pay—mainly because their income is necessary. Most women like working outside the home, as it gives them money of their own, more varied activities, a larger circle of friends, and higher self-esteem. But it often creates a double burden for them, since housekeeping and child care are still considered mainly women's responsibilities. Some couples are working out schedules to share domestic tasks, but others may quarrel about it, let the woman do all the work in the home, or break up.

Money is a major area of conflict in marriage, not only where it is in short supply, but also where it represents power in the relationship. Sex and children run a close second and third as areas of dispute. While some couples have experimented with "open marriage," meaning they permit each other to have sexual relations with other people, for the majority, feelings of betrayal and jealousy tend to cause conflict if extramarital relations occur. Since sexual fulfillment has become a recognized goal now for women as well as men, the double standard is being challenged. This can increase the possibility of conflict.

Finally, children can bring problems as well as joy into a marriage. Most parents love their children deeply, but living with them and with each other is sometimes difficult. There can be jealousy, competition for love, disagreements on how to raise children, extra strain on the family budget, and physical illness multiplied. Studies show that married people are happiest with each other before children are born and after the last one leaves home. In the modern world, children are expensive. In pre-modern times, children were assets, even necessities for families. And parents were not expected to focus so exclusively on the needs of their children. Nor were adult caretakers of children so isolated from other adults. Our society does not always make it easy for parents to care for their children adequately. Adults—mainly mothers—who stay at home to take care of their children are isolated in their small nuclear families, often far from other relatives. In families where both parents work outside the home, inadequate or expensive day care and the double burden for women of housework and paid work create other frustrations.

Although children, money, and sex may be areas of conflict in marriages of all classes, there are some class differences in both the nature and resolution of conflict. Among the upper class, there is somewhat less divorce, though this does not mean that marriages are necessarily happier. Rather, families of great wealth that merge have an interest in keeping marriages intact. The divorce rate is highest among the working class and the poor. This is partly due to the fact that people marry earlier in these classes, and the younger people are when they marry, the more likely they are to divorce.[83] While the median age of marriage is now twenty-four for men and twenty-one for women, it is three years lower at the lowest socioeconomic levels and three years higher at the top.[84] In addition, families with less money have more material problems, and this may create added tensions and frustrations within the family.

But the institution of marriage persists. For all its difficulties, it provides many satisfactions. Marriage is still the main legally sanctified way to live together and have children. For many people, that legal and social recognition is important. Marriage is a way to formalize and legitimize a long-term relationship with a member of the opposite sex. Marriage can look attractive in a world where it is often difficult to have a full social life as a single person. In our insecure world, marriage appears, to many, to be the surest guarantee of physical caring, psychological support, sexual fulfillment, and personal importance. As partners overcome difficulties together and mature, their love for each other may deepen. They may find companionship in play and grief and simple daily living. A good marriage can provide intimacy, sharing secrets, enjoying friends, just being together, even silently.

Marriage persists not only because it satisfies certain needs. It also persists because it is difficult to change any institution. Marriage is familiar. Most of us grew up believing it was the natural way to spend adulthood. It is difficult to undo years of socialization.

Many of the needs that marriage fulfills, however, can be met in other ways. Some people choose not to marry. They attempt to find companionship, joy, support, and intimacy in other relationships.

Choosing Not to Marry. Some dramatic changes in living arrangements occurred in the 1970s. The number of people of the opposite sex living together without being married more than doubled from 1970 to 1978. This increase was predominately among the young. Eight times as many people under the age of twenty-five cohabited in 1978 as compared to in 1970.

And, in seven out of ten of the unmarried-couple households, both partners were under the age of forty-five. Another trend of the 1970s was a large—43 percent—increase in the numbers of families in which no men were present.[85] And the number of single-person households also increased significantly in the first eight years of the decade: in 1978, one out of every five households consisted of just one person. This was a 42 percent increase since 1970. Although most people who live alone are elderly widows, more and more young people are living in single-person households. From 1970 to 1978, the largest increase in people living alone came among people under the age of thirty-four.[86]

Why, given all the social pressure to marry, do so many people resist it? One answer, of course, is that some do not. It is part of the life cycle to be unmarried for a certain time as an adult, and today many such people live alone rather than with parents or other relatives. Some of these young people are waiting a bit longer than they used to before getting married. Some would like to marry, but don't because they cannot find a suitable partner. However, for more and more people, living alone is becoming a chosen way of life. This includes people who have never married and those formerly married but now divorced or widowed. The reasons for their choice are varied. Many career-oriented women fear that a family would hold them back, and they can support themselves today outside of marriage more easily than in the past. Some men prefer to buy the services of a housekeeper and not bind themselves to permanent personal relationships. Freer attitudes toward sexuality make the choice of a single life more attractive now. And many people no longer idealize marriage. Some people who had previously lived in close relationships report they like the freedom and independence of living alone. They have a wider circle of friends and more varied activities than before. By contrast, they describe living with one person over a long period of time as boring, an obstacle to self-development, hindering travel and new friendships; in short, entrapping. Here are some testimonies:

I love it. I'm very busy but I've always enjoyed being busy and I feel that I can extend myself in each area adequately. Sometimes I feel that I don't

have enough time for one thing or another, but in general I feel that I
have enough time for myself, enough time for friends, enough time to
take care of my work, enough time to be with my children.[87]

Right now I'm working at becoming my own person. I think there are
some areas in becoming myself that I probably missed by becoming
married at twenty-two. I don't think I was a fully developed person....
I want to be certain I'm sure of me before I become involved with
another person. I think I would lose touch with myself.[88]

But single people, too, get the blues sometimes. The world is
very "coupled." Social events are often planned around couples,
partly because a single person may bring a threat of sexual
competition. So, many singles feel lonely. Here is what these
people say:

I sometimes feel as if I have two heads. If you're single and you're a
parent—well, you don't fit into a studio flat in the city with the kids and
you don't fit out here [in the suburbs] without a husband.[89]

You're really on a shelf. As a widow, you're put into a little box and that's
it. Goodbye. Nobody discusses it with you.[90]

Some people do not choose to live alone or to be married, as is
evidenced by the over one million households that consist of
two unrelated adults of the opposite sex. In addition, the number
of same-sex, unrelated persons living together as roommates and
as homosexual couples has increased significantly.

The validity of unions of unmarried heterosexual couples is
beginning to be recognized. Recently, a California court awarded
$104,000 to Michelle Triola in partial recognition of her claim
on the actor Lee Marvin, with whom she lived for six years,
unmarried. And the New Jersey Supreme Court ruled on June 25,
1979, that promises made between two people living together
can constitute a legal and binding contract.[91]

There is no accurate statistic on the number of homosexual
couples because discrimination forces many lesbians and gay
men into secrecy. Those who are parents may fear they will lose
custody of their children: being homosexual is reason enough for
some courts to take custody away. There is now an active gay
male and lesbian rights movement which has won some impor-

tant victories protecting civil liberties of homosexuals. Some lesbians and gay men live safely hidden in publicly heterosexual families. Others appear to be singles. But some live in self-chosen families of their own, as couples, and sometimes with children. Most of these relationships are lesbian, that is, between women. Fewer male homosexuals live in long-term unions and, like single heterosexual males, rarely have children living with them.[92]

Children in lesbian families are often raised with extra care. Many lesbian mothers, concerned for their children's sexual identity, take special pains to provide diverse experiences that include men. Often having left unhappy marriages, they try not to repeat oppressive male/female roles in their new relationship. Two mothers, sharing the work and nurturance of child care, may provide a more loving home than some heterosexual parents. Some lesbian mothers talk about being less torn between their children and their partners than they were with former male partners. One woman writes, "Alice never puts me into the corner of having to decide between my kids and her the way men used to. It has something to do with the way women relate to others, especially to children. There's more emotion involved."[93]

Yet a child with a homosexual parent may feel "strange" among peers. Even when people close to the child are supportive of a parent's homosexuality, the larger society is generally prejudiced against it. So anxiety about disclosure is something that many members of the homosexual family live with. Many lesbian and gay male parents have built supportive networks for themselves and their children that help deal with the prejudice they often face. And homosexual families—like all families—are quite diverse. Many of the same factors that result in differences in heterosexual families—class, race, ethnicity—can also make for different kinds of homosexual families.

Adoptive Families. Most adults choose the families they will live in. Children, of course, make no such choices. Most live with their biological parents. Of the 65 million children under age eighteen in the United States today, two out of three live with their two biological parents. Of the rest, a little under half live with one biological parent and one other adult, and a little over half live only with their mothers. One out of a hundred live with only their fathers. Three out of a hundred, approximately 2 million children, are cared for by adults who are not their biological parents.[94] What are their experiences of family?

Most children who don't live with a biological parent, live either with other kin or in adoptive families. When adoptive parents are warm and loving, children may hardly notice any difference between their family and that of other children living with biologically related parents. Many things affect the family experience of the adopted child, including the age at which she or he was adopted. Obviously, a child adopted as an infant has a different kind of family experience from one adopted at an older age. Should an adoptive parent tell the child the truth about her or his origin? Growing up knowing one is just about the only person around without even one biologically related parent can feel isolating. On the other hand, not telling a child about adoption may also be very hurtful. It is a hard secret to keep and others sometimes break the silence. Learning this truth is always a shock, and more so if the child has not been gently prepared for it.[95] Even with very caring adoptive parents, individuals often yearn to know who their biological parents are, in order to be clear about their own identity. Once they have grown up, some of them search for their biological parents. Social attitudes have everything to do with how children feel about being adopted. Where children are raised communally, for example, individual biological parents do not assume such overwhelming importance.

Children in Institutions. Fewer than 50,000 children in the United States live in institutions.[96] This is a far smaller proportion of the population than ever before, for several reasons: birthrates are down; parents live longer; and social welfare policies such as Aid to Families with Dependent Children allow more parents and children to stay together than in former times. Children in institutions live outside of the family. This can be a painful experience, if only because most people live within families. The institutional setting is more impersonal, the staff less involved with each individual child, the rules not adjusted to personality differences. One man remembered his years in an orphanage as being neither happy nor unhappy. They were not lonely; they were not warm. He said: "When you start off your life in an orphanage, you don't know there's any other kind of life. My childhood was really nothing."[97] A child may form a special attachment to a particular case-worker or nurse, but generally, growing up in an institution is a negative experience. Sometimes people living that way lose their zest for life, as shown by lower learning scores and a withdrawn, unloving manner. Group child rearing under different conditions need not be harmful. Children raised in group settings in countries like Austria, Cuba, Israel, Poland, the Soviet Union, and Yugoslavia seem to be as well adjusted as children raised in traditional family settings.[98] In most of these situations, children do have some contact with parents or other kin.

The main difference between institutions that work well or poorly for the people in them is the material and social support the society gives them. This support depends on attitudes toward the nonprivate rearing of children. In the United States today, these attitudes are still mostly negative, and children are adopted, if possible, or at least placed in temporary foster homes. The private solution is preferred.

The Last Difference. As branches emerge from trees—or new families form out of old ones—what happens to those "old" families? And what will happen when the new families of today become tomorrow's old families? A recent news report begins, "A quietly ticking social time bomb—America's rapidly aging population—is due to explode in twenty years or so."[99] It goes on to say that the average life expectancy has gone up about ten years since 1940 and is now about sixty-nine years for men and seventy-seven years for women. Many more people are living beyond age eighty. In 1976, there were about 22 million people over the age of sixty-five in the United States, or one out of every ten Americans.[100]

How do the aged live? Poorly. The typical after-tax income for a male head of household over age sixty-five is $5,764. The pretax median for this age group was $6,292, about half the median for a male head of household under sixty-five.[101] About 3.5 million, or 15 percent, live at or below the federally defined level of poverty for a family of two—that is, on an income of $3,711 or less per year.[102] In all, roughly one-third of the aged are poor, and since women live longer than men, most of the aged poor are female. Women's pensions are lower, based on their lower lifetime earnings; often women have no pensions at all. While pensions are boosted by Social Security payments, Medicare, Medicaid, food stamps, and housing subsidies, rapid inflation reduces the buying power of these fixed sources of income. A recent investigation showed that people on this level sometimes eat pet food to save money. And illness is chronic among the aged: one out of twenty are actually homebound.

Like most people, the aged usually live in a family: with each other as a "completed" family; with their brothers and sisters from their "root" family; or, less often, with their grown children. Some live alone. Only about 10 percent of those over the age of seventy-five are institutionalized, and most who are, are past eighty.[103]

Of course, "home" will look different for the old of different classes. Wealth can buy the best medical care, replacement of damaged parts, and around-the-clock service. Upper-class people can probably stay in their own homes until they die, or they can move to another of the family's homes in a mild climate. Their wealth and the power of their will and testament may compel respect from their children and grandchildren until they die. Those in the upper middle class may also prolong their lives through good care, and they may buy property in a comfortable retirement community. Such old people often continue to help their adult children, since they have the means—money, or business or professional contacts. In any case, they are not themselves dependents. Others in the middle and working classes plunge into poverty on retirement and cannot afford even a small apartment. Some live in small furnished rooms. Others move in with relatives. These dependent poor may be well loved by those who care for them, but without adequate social services, the emotional and financial strain on the small nuclear unit often leads to mere toleration at best. No wonder most old people cling to their independence as long as possible.

Growing old alone is hard, and growing old together with a partner is also hard. Watching someone disappear, slowly or quickly, hurts and reminds one of one's own approaching death. Old people are lonely, not only because their friends and relatives die, but also because our society isolates them and does not value them. Loneliness affects individuals differently. Some get angry and hurt their mates. Quibbling over slim resources may make an ageing couple bitter. Furthermore, retired men often experience a sudden feeling of having dropped out from life, which women don't experience in the same way, even if they have worked for pay. This is probably due to the fact that a woman never completely retires. Her housework does not come to an end. If men do more housework after retirement, they may feel humiliated, and women may feel their turf invaded. On the other hand, an old couple may putter about happily together, free at last to enjoy their leisure. The old tensions gone, they may draw closer together. Old couples, like all couples, vary. How they live and feel depends on their health, their income, and their relations with the surrounding community.

Growing old will mean different things depending on whether one lives alone or with a partner. It will also probably be different for lesbians than it is for heterosexual women. One woman writes that although the physical ageing process is difficult for all people, because of different cultural norms, "ageism is not as much of a problem" among lesbians. She believes, however, that there is not yet a real community for older lesbians, and she speaks of the need for building such a community.[104]

Among older people, relationships with children who have grown up and moved away are quite various, and some of this has to do with who is dependent on whom. For the majority, relations with children and grandchildren are an important link to the present and the future. Here grandmothers seem to be in a better position than grandfathers. They can be child-minders and feel useful and important in the motherly role. Grandfathers spend time with grandchildren too, but they more often feel distant.[105]

In almost all families, women hold the network of kin together through all generations, by visits, telephone calls, mutual services, and so on. Mothers and daughters are especially likely to keep in close touch. Daughters, more than sons, become the main caretakers of the elderly, as they are of children. Men serve their parents more with money than with direct care. Therefore, the worst in-law conflicts arise between the mothers and wives of men, not only because of jealousy, but also over material needs, if each one has a household to maintain. Problems also arise when one generation has a different set of values and life-styles from another, which is likely in a population that has migrated from the country to the city or from another land.

The problems faced by the aged in the United States are due as much to the way this society organizes existence as to the biological fact of growing older. Inequalities of wealth and power, and private solutions to physical and social problems, mark our path from the cradle to the grave. All of this experience could be structured differently. Just as there is no "natural" reason to have separate classes, to separate one racial or ethnic group from another, to reward one gender less well than another, so there is no rationality in separating one generation from another. Divided, people may turn against or away from one another. United, they can help enrich each others' lives. Old people who are still vigorous and alert could remain integrated within their communities to everyone's advantage. They could continue using the skills developed over many years to do their chosen work. They could participate in helpful activities, such as tutoring and caring for children. While science may outstrip the "wisdom" of the past, human support is still indispensable. Needed and valued, old people could be assets rather than liabilities and could enjoy life longer, not merely wait it out. They would be strangers no more.

Of course, even today, some old people do achieve this ideal. Sometimes they do it within their traditional families; sometimes they form new families of their own. A small number of old people, like some young people, have found that communal living can provide companionship and support, while allowing individuals to maintain their independence. The communal alternative is not a new one; it is known in other cultures and other eras, as the next chapter shows. A commune of like-minded people, young and old, democratically running their collective, caring for one another like family while avoiding some of the most oppressive family relations, is the ideal model for some. Can it really exist for large numbers of us? Or will we move toward a modified, more satisfying version of the nuclear family? Only the future will tell, and the future is very open; frightening sometimes, but inviting, too.

THREE: The Search for Alternatives

Past, Present, and Future

By Amy Swerdlow and Phyllis Vine

THE FAMILY IS NEITHER a static nor a uniform institution. As the first two chapters of this book have indicated, family forms have changed over time and vary with class, race, ethnicity, and religion. We have seen how household organization and family networks evolve through the interaction of economic, political, and cultural institutions—and how the family, in turn, shapes these institutions. It is not surprising, therefore, that in every age and stage of Western history, social planners who were attempting to create a better society found themselves experimenting with alternatives to traditional family structures. Self-conscious and purposeful attempts to restructure marriage and child-rearing patterns have been part of a long tradition of utopian and communitarian struggles to abolish hierarchy, inequality, exploitation, and competition in economic, political, and social institutions. In the past two centuries, communitarian societies have frequently attempted to create freer relations and provide greater equality between the sexes and to minimize the biological parents' control over the lives of young children.

This chapter describes a variety of attempts to establish alternative household and family forms. As we examine these alternatives, we will find that economic, political, and social conditions shape radical intentional alternatives, just as they influence the normative family. Even those who criticize their own society are children of that society and cannot always free themselves of the political assumptions and the value system into which they were born.

Some of the earliest utopian proposals for the radical transformation of sexual and child-rearing practices, notably Plato's *Republic,* written in the fourth century B.C. and Tomasso Campanella's *The City of the Sun,* published two thousand years later, were based on the conviction that the private economic interests of the patriarchal household compete with the welfare of the state. But other communitarian experiments with alternative family structures, particularly in the nineteenth century, were motivated more by concern for the welfare of the individual than by the needs of the state. The belief that people can improve their life on earth and assure their place in heaven by creating communities superior to those of their forebears has been part of the American consciousness from the time the Pilgrims landed at Plymouth Rock. The promise of the freedom of an open continent, without entrenched political institutions, led to the creation of hundreds of utopian communities in America in the late eighteenth and nineteenth centuries. These communities, both secular and religious in purpose, rejected social inequality, harsh labor conditions, political and economic exploitation, competition, materialism, and individualism. A significant number were also concerned with ending the domination of women by men, establishing freer relations between parents and children, and loosening the bonds of monogamous marriage.

By the twentieth century, the rise of large corporate monopolies, the alienation of labor, the growth of consumerism, and the physical pressures or urban living have prompted thousands of women and men, many of them middle-class youth, to create communities that attempt to reduce social alienation and provide emotional fulfillment in personal relations. Challenging the materialism and wastefulness of the affluent society, some have turned to extended family arrangements based on shared interests, cooperative values, and emotional support, rather than on biological and legal ties.

The emergence of the second wave of American feminism in the 1960s and 1970s has prompted a growing number of people to experiment with forms that allow maximum opportunities for the creation of equality between women and men in all areas of sexual and domestic activity, including housework and child care. The dramatic increase in the number of women working in the paid labor force in the second half of this century has created millions of nuclear households with two parents working outside the home. This phenomenon, plus the rising number of single-parent families, has called for alterations in the way household work is organized, for new family structures, and for new definitions of the family and a reexamination of its ideology. Changes in household composition and household roles raise difficult problems that, in the United States, people are attempting to solve on an individual or communal basis. In some other nations, however, government policies are being developed, particularly in the areas of child care and domestic maintenance, to support the changing nuclear unit.

The alternatives to be explored in this chapter are aimed at creating a better human environment and more fulfilling emotional relations between men and women, adults and children. Whether these familial experiments are viewed as successes or failures, whether they seem to liberate or oppress, whether they seem exciting or dreary, they serve as reminders that the family is a malleable institution.

Families are in flux, responding and reacting to a changing world. Knowledge of intentional alternatives proposed in the past, and those that are being lived today, may help to sharpen our insights regarding those aspects of family life we wish to retain and those we wish to alter or discard. It helps us to see that in order to change the family, we have to make certain changes in the larger society—in work relations and in government policies. Looking at what others have dreamed, and what some have achieved, may provide a sense that people can play a conscious and active role, not only in shaping their own families, but in creating the family ideology of the future.

Models from the Past

Throughout human history, people have dreamed of a perfect society. The nature of this earthly paradise has varied a great deal over time, as concepts of pleasure, freedom, and love have changed. What is considered ideal has also varied depending on the economic, social, and political position of those advocating the new order. For some, creating a powerful and productive state has been the goal; for others, eliminating exploitation and inequality has been paramount. Some people have attempted to realize their dreams through revolution, others through visionary schemes committed to paper, and still others by withdrawing from the larger society to create their own perfect enclaves.[1]

Creating a Superior State. As early as the fourth century B.C. in ancient Athens, the philosopher Plato noted that families of the citizen class were too engrossed in competition for wealth and power to concern themselves with the general welfare. In *The Republic,* he proposed that an elite group of talented people called the Guardians devote themselves to ruling and serving the Greek city-state. For this group of women and men, the strong kinship ties of the biological family would have to be abolished, along with monogamous marriage and the patriarchal household. To utilize the talents of women as well as men, the traditional division of sex roles, which in Athens kept women confined to the home, would also have to be revised. Plato proposed that men and women of the Guardian class be encouraged to mate, not according to their inclination, but according to scientific principles. This is called eugenic breeding and requires the selection of sexual partners who possess physical and mental traits that the society defines as desirable. Eugenic group breeding in Plato's Republic would take place at special ceremonial festivals. The parents of a particular festival would be considered the mothers and fathers of all the children born of that festival and, likewise, the children of the festival would consider themselves brothers and sisters. To ensure that parents would not favor their own biological offspring to the detriment of the state, and that children would form no special attachments to their parents or siblings, newborn infants would be placed in communal nurseries at the moment of birth. Precautions would be taken so that mothers would not be able to identify their own children even when the babies were brought to the women for nursing.

In order to develop the talents of all capable individuals, Plato planned to give women the same educational opportunities as men. Freed from domestic responsibilities and child care, Guardian women would participate fully in political and social life. Although Plato's proposals challenged the Greek customs that confined female citizens to the home under strict control of fathers, husbands, brothers, or sons, the principal goal of *The Republic* was not to liberate women. Plato merely wished to utilize their brains and breeding function in the interest of making Athens more powerful. Women of the lower classes, according to Plato's plan, would still live under the rule of men and be responsible for the domestic work, not only for their own families, but for the Guardian class as well.

Nearly two thousand years after Plato conceived his Republic, an English statesman, Sir Thomas More, presented to his contemporaries the tale of a voyage to an imaginary and ideal island community. Writing in 1516, More was inspired by the discovery of the Americas and by his reading of Plato. He wanted to invent a perfect community, not so much as a myth of a distant paradise, but as a critique of his own society and as a model for reform. More called his island "Utopia," a name which derives from two Latin words meaning "no place" and "good place." So outlandish, yet so appealing, was the social system that More described that the word "utopia" came to mean all forms of unattainable perfection.

While More boldly eliminated private property and money as a medium of exchange in his imaginary society, he did not destroy the patriarchal family as Plato had proposed to do. More maintained the monogamous, extended paternalistic family as the basis for production and biological reproduction. Although More rejected many of the most abusive injustices of his own society, he was very much a man of his time. He accepted slavery as a legitimate economic practice and did not challenge most of the contemporary assumptions regarding male-female relations and sex roles. In the fictional Utopia, premarital sexual intercourse and adultery are punished severely because, according to More, "few people would join in married love—with confinement to a single partner and all the petty annoyances that married love involves—unless they were strictly restrained from a life of promiscuity."[2] Although private families remain the basic economic and biological unit in More's Utopia, some communal structures exist as well. Dining and cooking facilities are shared by groups of thirty households, and younger children eat separately in a group nursery.

The Italian Renaissance philosopher Tomasso Campanella, while continuing the search for the powerful and perfect state, in 1623 made plans for a communal "City of the Sun" that would completely eliminate monogamous marriage and the household organized around the biological family. In Campanella's literary utopia, sexual arrangements would be made, not to serve the physical or emotional needs of the individual, but in the cause of eugenics, the scientific breeding of human beings to improve the race. His goal, like Plato's, was to create a superior race of people who would be devoted to the welfare of the state and the ruling class.

While women remain in secondary status, controlled by a priest and three male magistrates, in City of the Sun no individual woman is completely dependent on, or controlled by, a father or husband. If such a social system had ever been attempted, the role of women might have been transformed as their interaction and solidarity would have cut across family lines. But in his own time, Campanella's antifamilial proposals were largely ignored. In fact, his entire authoritarian, monarchist social outlook could find little acceptance in a society turning to commerce, the promotion of individual rights, and the institutionalization of the nuclear family based on private property and heterosexual love.

The Pursuit of Happiness. In the eighteenth century a philosophical movement called the Enlightenment, stressing science and progress, led to a new wave of utopian visions in the nineteenth century. The Enlightenment's emphasis on reason and on human ability to control the physical and social environment brought forth not only literary visions of new social orders, but hundreds of actual alternative family experiments as well. The goal of most nineteenth-century utopian planners and thinkers was to create a social environment in which the harsh industrial process could be humanized and economic exploitation minimized. Each individual would be given the right to education, leisure, and joyful work. In the early stages of industrialization, economic and social institutions seemed malleable. Utopian planners were optimistic about their ability to escape from the factory system and the commercial order by building their own communities. They believed these would serve as models for the whole society.

Two utopian leaders of the nineteenth century who were particularly concerned with improving the quality of workers' lives were Robert Owen, an Englishman, and Charles Fourier, a Frenchman. Both Owen and Fourier recognized that family arrangements, sexual relations, and child-rearing customs were central concerns in the creation of a humanistic society.

Robert Owen made a fortune in the British textile industry in the nineteenth century. Born in 1771, the son of an ironmonger and saddler, he left home at the age of ten to begin work as a draper's apprentice. He moved from one venture to another until he became one of the most powerful industrialists in Britain. As his power and wealth grew, so did his social conscience, his dissatisfaction with industrialization, and his concern for common people. Owen was appalled by the working and living conditions of urban factory laborers. Convinced that character was influenced by environment, he proposed the creation of planned communities in which decent working conditions, education, leisure, and cultural facilities would lead to joyful work and greater productivity.

When Owen's efforts to promote communal settlements in England were rejected by Parliament, he turned his attention to the open spaces and the promise of a free society in America. The first commune he established in the new world was located on the Wabash River in Indiana, on a site he had purchased in 1825 from a religious communitarian sect, the Rappites. The goal of New Harmony, according to Owen, was "to change from the individual to the social system; from single families with separate interests to communities of many families with one interest."[4]

Owen attributed the fragmentation and competitiveness of industrial capitalist society largely to the institution of the private family. In it he found not only selfishness, but the source of social oppression and man's tyranny over woman. He attacked monogamous marriage and encouraged people to end unhappy unions by promising them that their children would be cared for by a community of peers should they decide to separate. Owen was an early proponent of birth control, believing that men and women would enjoy more loving sexual relations if women were freed from the fear of frequent pregnancies.

Although New Harmony was short-lived and could not fulfill all of Owen's communal dreams, it did succeed in establishing cooperative dining facilities, kitchens, and laundries. An experimental school for ninety boys was established in which the pupils, regardless of their parents' wealth, supported themselves through their own labor and produced enough surplus to pay for their education.

All persons in New Harmony were dealt with as individuals and credited with the value of their services daily. The costs of housing, fuel, washing, medical attention, and schooling were debited from each member's account. Such arrangements decreased the influence of the biological family as an economic and social unit.

As women worked with men at certain jobs, they adopted the new jacket and pantalette costume which was provoking scorn and ridicule in conventional circles all over America.[5] This "bloomer" costume was considered by feminists of the time to be a symbol of woman's rights. The tight long skirts and heavy corsets being worn by most women hampered circulation and movement, thus demonstrating their oppression.

Visitors flocked to see the experiment in New Harmony, considered by intellectuals and radicals to be a wonder of the Western world. Though the New Harmony community collapsed in less than two years, it influenced hundreds of Americans and Europeans who founded at least sixteen other Owenite communes in the United States. In all of them, collective cooking, communal dining, and cooperative child care were combined with cooperative agricultural and industrial labor.

Owen's proposals for modification of family practice and sexual relations were considered radical and even immoral in his day. Some, such as divorce and birth control, have since achieved wide acceptance. But Owen's conviction that the family is a powerful, autonomous institution in society, more important in dictating the quality of life than the economic system or class relations, has been challenged by succeeding generations of social theorists.

Among those influenced by visits to New Harmony and by the writings of Robert Owen was Frances Wright, a free-thinking woman who organized Nashoba, the first interracial commune in the United States. Wright, who had been born in Britain, was a frequent visitor to America. In setting up Nashoba, she combined two radical interests: opposition to slavery and a belief in the rights of women. In 1825-26, she purchased a tract of land in Nashoba, Tennessee, and procured a group of slaves whom she planned to prepare for eventual liberation by improving their education and providing them with the experience of working for pay. Wright also encouraged free Negroes with children to join her colony. She hoped that by placing slaves, free blacks, and whites together, "the amalgamation of the races" would take place in "good taste with good feeling."

To attempt to liberate slaves in the 1820s in the United States was a dangerously unpopular cause. Many in the South opposed Wright's program. But conventional public opinion in the North found most shocking Wright's domestic and sexual reforms. Frances Wright declared that the marriage laws existing outside of Nashoba would have no force in her colony. No man would be permitted to assert right or power over any woman. Nor, on the other hand, could women assert claims to the companionship or the protection of any man, "beyond what mutual inclination dictates." Wright totally outraged public opinion when she declared: "Let us enquire—not if a mother be a wife, or a father, a husband—but if parents can supply, to the creatures they have brought into being, all things requisite to make existence a blessing."[6]

An evangelical and abolitionist journal published an account of Nashoba by one of its white leaders that invoked the wrath of even those sympathetic to the liberation of slaves. The writer stated that slaves were being taught that the proper basis for sexual intercourse was the unrestrained choice of both parties. Responding to charges that Nashoba was little more than a brothel, Frances Wright modified the community and then dissolved it by transporting the slaves to Haiti, where they were emancipated.

Although Wright reflected some of the white prejudices of her time in trying to remake slaves in her own Anglo-Saxon image, her experiment stands out as the only effort to address both race and sex relations in an American communitarian society. Most utopian communes in America were planned by, and attracted, white Anglo-Saxon Protestants: workers, farmers, small businessmen, and professionals. These were the kinds of people who became followers of Charles Fourier in America and who set up a number of secular communes in the 1830s and 1840s all over the United States.

Fourier was the son of a wealthy French merchant, but he had lost his inheritance in the upheavals of the French Revolution. A lonely and solitary man, he dreamed of a socially integrated, joyful, conflict-free society he called Harmony. In Harmony, physical deprivation, class conflict, and revolution would be abolished. True gratification of all human passions and desires would lead not only to happiness, but to productive work and industrial progress as well. Fourier spent close to forty years planning a fantastic blueprint for a community he called a Phalanx. The Phalanx, according to Fourier's vision, would consist of exactly 1,620 people who would be housed in an elaborate, luxurious complex. An urban structure in an agricultural setting would provide living space, workshops, cultural facilities, and play areas. In this enclosed space, which would be larger than the palace at Versailles, Phalanx members would live together in a system of free love, equality between the sexes, and collective care for children. Among the major human passions, Fourier believed love fared the worst in civilization because it was given no outlet but marriage. He was also critical of heterosexuality as the only acceptable sexual relationship, pointing out that in many earlier societies, particularly Sparta, young men had been encouraged to practice sodomy as "the path to virtue."

In Fourier's imaginary Harmony, as in Owen's communities, all persons would be dealt with as individuals, not as family members. Even children five years old would be the owners of the fruits of their labor, which would be held in trust for them. At a time when child labor was widespread and fathers controlled the earnings of both wives and children, Fourier's acceptance of the child as an autonomous person was utopian indeed.

Fourier developed a system he called "passional attraction" which placed people in work and social groups according to their sensual or emotional compatability. He even invented a time-table to indicate when certain passions would be in equilibrium. Fourier worked out elaborately contrived courts of love. There, men and women of the Phalanx could play out countless amorous pageants and erotic games and form sexual combinations designed to fulfill every fantasy and every urge. In his advocacy of sexual release, Fourier might today be considered a precursor of Sigmund Freud and Wilhelm Reich. It is interesting to note, however, that unlike Freud and Reich, Fourier had little interest in or understanding of children's sexuality. He classified children as the third sex and denied them any outlets or access to the courts of love until they reached adolescence. But because he believed that all work could be pleasurable if it made use of a person's need for sensual gratification, he suggested that young children would enjoy the task of cleaning out toilets, something adults despise.

Fourier attracted a large number of followers in the United States who created approximately forty different communes in the 1840s. But only three lasted for more than two years. None could measure up to Fourier's elaborate architectural and institutional blueprint, and none ever attempted to carry out his sexual and passional schemes.

While the ideas of Owen and Fourier helped expand the nineteenth-century commune movement in the United States, some of the most innovative and long-lived communitarian societies were religious in inspiration. Seeking to create a community of spiritual perfection, a piece of the Kingdom of God on earth, the Shakers, the Oneidans, and the Mormons all rejected the monogamous couple and the nuclear family in their religious communities. This they did for different reasons based on their own particular interpretations of the Bible.

The Shakers, who believed that the Second Coming of Christ had already taken place, practiced celibacy because they believed that sexual abstinence was the rule in heaven. Ann Lee, the founder of the Shaker sect and its prophet, had herself suffered a series of painful and unwanted pregnancies. She and her followers, many of whom were women, were no doubt also attracted to celibacy because it freed women from sexual exploitation. Men and women lived separately in Shaker villages. Punishment for physical contact between the sexes was expulsion. Physical pleasure was derived from whirling, shaking dances that led to ecstatic abandonment to God—hence the name Shakers. The Shaker theology held that men and women were equals, a belief that led to some equalization in work assignments for women and for men. On the whole, however, work was divided along conventional sex lines, with women serving as personal cleaners and menders for particular men with whom they had no physical contact or personal relationship.

The Mormons, on the other hand, were convinced by their reading of the Bible that God wished man to take several wives. Mormon leaders in the Utah territory lived in extended polygamous families until the United States government forced them to abandon this practice as a condition for Utah's becoming a state. Such regulation of the sexual and marriage customs of a religious group is an example of the way governments regulate family forms and define what people perceive as "the norm."

In Oneida, founded in 1848 in upstate New York by John Humphrey Noyes, monogamy was condemned as a sinful practice, a form of ownership of one person by another. Noyes and his followers believed that in the eyes of God, all men and women are husbands and wives to each other. Oneidans developed an alternative sexual arrangement they called "Complex Marriage," which evoked suspicion, hostility, and outrage in the larger community. To their critics' charges that Complex Marriage was a form of free love both immoral and illegal, Noyes and his followers replied that their practice was neither adulterous nor promiscuous. In fact, there was no real free choice of sexual partners as Oneida required that a selection committee consisting of male elders make decisions regarding the pairing of women and men for sexual encounters. The committee was instructed to refuse to match couples who appeared to be making exclusive or enduring commitment to each other.

Noyes's theocratic philosophy was based on the belief that the pious male was responsible for the spiritual welfare of the community. This philosophy was extended to birth control, which was achieved without abstinence, through male continence, in Oneida. This practice, in which men stopped themselves from ejaculating during sexual intercourse, was one of the first forms of birth control in modern times that placed responsibility on the male. It was also intended to allow women to enjoy greater pleasure during sexual intercourse.

The Oneidans' practice of male continence was such an effective means of birth control, that for the first twenty years only about forty infants were born into the community. At a time when the average white middle-class family included between four and five children, Oneidan women were bearing one or two each. Then, in the 1860s, to guarantee that only women and men who were the most "perfect" would bear the community's children, a form of population control and eugenic breeding was undertaken in Oneida. This was called "stirpiculture," from the Latin word for branch. Stirpiculture required that the supervisory committee which coupled men and women for sexual intercourse also select those who would bear the community's children. Between 1869 and 1879, fifty-eight stirpiculture children were born in Oneida.

Oneidans objected to ownership in any form, not only the exclusivity of husbands and wives. Collective ownership of property and labor was a governing principle, and the entire community shared the domestic tasks that would have been the responsibility of individuals or family units in the outside society. While each individual had her or his private sleeping quarters, cooking and eating occurred in a communal kitchen and dining room, and recreation took place in a building called "the mansion."

Consistent with their collective mode of production and reproduction was the communal organization of all aspects of child care. Children were the responsibility of the entire community, not of their biological parents alone. Infants remained under their mother's care until weaned at the age of twelve to eighteen months. At that time, they went to live with their peers in the Children's House. The adults of both sexes assumed the social role of mothering and fathering for all the children. Special affection on the part of the biological parents was scorned. Women who were thought to be too indulgent as mothers, or men who were thought to be too exacting and severe as fathers, were expected to subjugate their own inclinations for the selfless purpose of communal child rearing.

Communal child rearing in Oneida affected the lives of each person on a daily basis. It lessened the exclusive responsibility and authority of individual parents over their children. For the children, this meant nurturance and attention from numbers of adults. And children did not have to adjust their needs and aspirations solely to the requirements of their biological mothers or fathers. Parents, similarly, did not have to sacrifice all their own needs and interests to support their offspring. By having all the adults care for all the children, people in Oneida distinguished between biological and social parenting and involved the entire community in child rearing. Mothers and fathers were not isolated in individual households. Communal structures allowed for frequent, meaningful interaction with other adults and children.

Like child care, housework was also a group endeavor. As one person who was raised in the community noted, "Small groups of people worked side by side...and they were able to talk with each other as they worked."[7] Shared work included such domestic chores as gardening, canning foods from the fields, and washing clothes.

Though domestic chores were most often done by women, thus continuing some of the sexual stereotypes of the society outside, women and men worked side by side in several industries which the community developed. When Oneida decided to begin manufacturing silk, two women and one man were sent to a nearby factory to learn the skill. Elsewhere, women worked alongside men at the lathe in the machine shop, as typesetters in the printing shop, and as accountants and bookkeepers. The Oneida Circular, the community newspaper, was edited by a woman.

In some important ways, Oneida advanced the status of women above the level of contemporary society. It gave them a greater degree of control over their own sexual lives than was allowed to their contemporaries and also provided freedom from unwanted childbearing and from the isolation and drudgery of housework. But the Oneida ideology of male moral and ethical superiority, and the repression of woman's intimate connection with her children, gave women no area of life under their own control. Louis J. Kern, in an insightful article on sexuality and women in Oneida, points out that the attempts of the women of Oneida in the 1870s to return to monogamy and the nuclear family were due to their alienation from any other sources of status or power.[8]

Reorganizing the Private Home. Utopian societies that separated themselves from the mainstream were not the only places where changes in the organization of family and household were being proposed. Without directly challenging the integrity of the nuclear unit, another group of nineteenth-century reformers proposed alternatives to prevailing household organization. Their goal was to eliminate the tedious duplication of effort and the social isolation of daily housework in the nuclear family. These critics—educated middle-class women such as Melusina Fay Peirce and Charlotte Perkins Gilman— were responding to the fact that women's status and economic importance were decreasing as the separation broadened between production and consumption in industrial America.

In the second half of the nineteenth century, Melusina Fay Peirce and a group of Boston women and men attempted to use new technological advances in industry to bring efficiency, economic compensation, and status to the task of housework. They proposed a reorganization of the private home. Instead of the individual housewife, a collective organization of domestic workers would be employed for greater efficiency and social interaction. Pierce suggested that neighborhood associations be organized to perform domestic tasks cooperatively and that housing be redesigned to include communal kitchens, laundries, and eating facilities.[9] This proposal, widely discussed in the

1870s and 1880s, influenced Edward Bellamy's famous utopian novel, *Looking Backward*. Peirce argued that the individuals—presumably women—who would perform the domestic services for a number of households should be paid, just as workers outside the home were. Housework, performed cooperatively, would no longer be a "labor of love."

Thirty years later, Charlotte Perkins Gilman, the outstanding feminist theorist of her day, analyzed the domestic experience of women. In *The Home*, written in 1903, Gilman calculated that for 200 families there were 200 women who cooked an average of 6 hours a day (before modern refrigeration and electric appliances), or a total of 1,200 hours of labor for each day that these families had three meals. In addition, she estimated that if these individuals had been paid, it would have cost a total of $240 a day in wages, the equivalent of $1.20 a day per family at a time in America when the typical unskilled worker earned about $10 a week. She added, "Of course, if these cooks are housewives, they do not get the money."[10]

A critic of the double standard for women, Gilman wrote a satiric utopian novel, *Herland*, in 1915 to expose the folly of society's gender codes.[11] Herland is an all-woman society which had been isolated for centuries on a lush, lost island. Three American college men who "discover" this bucolic paradise are held captive by women who explain their society. The men learn that the barbarities of war and conflict had killed all the men more than two thousand years before, leaving women to reproduce themselves without men, through parthenogenesis. The people of Herland live in universal peace and mutual affection. The struggle over economic well-being, social mobility, job security, slums, ill housing, and disease has no place in their lives. Neither does the domestic conflict that Gilman observed in her own society. Because each of the women is a mother to her own children and to all the others, Motherhood had become a religion and a joy, not a burden or a gift to fathers and husbands. Working throughout the country, inhabitants of Herland have no single home in which they live all the time. Children are raised communally and nursed by their mothers for the first two years of life. After that they are socialized to extend

mother love to the entire society, which recognizes no differences in status or personal achievement. All competition and
selfishness were eliminated in the social process. Nor did the
limitations or privileges of gender codes apply to Herland. There,
all tasks are performed solely by women and regarded as equally
important as they benefit all.

Gilman's single-sex utopia has women doing all of the work,
even work that would have been expected of men in contemporary society. In *Herland,* Charlotte Perkins Gilman illustrates
how gender and family are constructions of the society of which
they are a part. By poking fun at some of the excesses of our
cultural stereotypes, she allowed readers to question and pose alternatives.

Scientific Socialism. By the end of the nineteenth century,
optimism about communitarian solutions to social problems
was waning. As dozens of communes in the United States and in
Europe dissolved due to internal strife, it was becoming apparent
that communal enclaves would not act as catalysts for the
transformation of the larger society. They were, in fact, suc-
cumbing to the very economic and social conditions they had
sought to reform. A growing number of dissatisfied intellectuals
and workers, seeking relief from the increasingly harsh labor and
living conditions engendered by the rapid expansion of industrial capitalism, now turned to a movement that sought not to
withdraw from society, but to overthrow it. This new communist movement, inspired by Karl Marx, a German political
economist and philosopher, proposed that throughout history
all political systems and forms of government were merely a
means for enforcing the economic exploitation of the masses by
a dominant class that owned the means of production.

According to the followers of Marx, owners and workers were
now locked in the final conflict of this age-old class struggle
which would lead eventually to a worldwide victory for the
working class and the establishment of socialism in the entire
society. A socialist economy, according to Marxists, would
create a classless society, free of private property, inequality, and
social injustice. Marxists rejected the assumptions of Owen and

Fourier that socialism could be achieved peacefully in isolated communities composed of well-intentioned individuals. Frederick Engels, a colleague and collaborator of Marx, characterized the followers of Owen and Fourier as "utopian socialists" because of their idealist approach to social change. He contrasted their visionary schemes with "scientific socialism," which called for working-class control not only of production but of the political system as well. Engels and Marx did, however, praise Fourier's poetic vision of a harmonious society and his desire to improve the life of workers. But they argued that it was naive and backward to believe, in the last quarter of the nineteenth century, that capitalism could be humanized through piecemeal reforms.

Marxists opposed the holding of private property and all relations of domination based on property. It is not surprising, therefore, that they condemned the patriarchal bourgeois family as a vehicle for the transmission of wealth and for the oppression of women by men. In *The Origin of the Family, Private Property and the State,* published in 1884, Engels described the transformation of the family from what he believed to be its earlier matrilineal and matrifocal form to its later patriarchal structure as "the world historical defeat of the female sex."[12] Marx, in an unpublished manuscript written in 1846, had declared that "the first division of labor is between man and woman for the propagation of children." To this Engels added: "The first class opposition that appears in history coincides with the development of antagonism between men and women in monogamous marriage, and the first class oppression coincides with that of the female sex by the male."[13] Although the patriarchal family and the oppression of women had preceded the capitalist system, Marxists promised that the overthrow of capitalism would bring an end to "the single family as a unit of society." Writing on what they called "the woman question," Engels and other Marxists predicted that in a socialist society women would leave unpaid, isolated domestic drudgery to work along with men in production outside the home. Private housekeeping would be transformed into a social industry, and the care and education of children would become a public affair.[14] Under socialism, motherhood would be a pleasure instead of a crushing responsibility, since all children, even those born out of wedlock, would be cared for by the society. With women no longer economically dependent upon men, sexual relations would be unconstrained and loving. Monogamous marriage, along with prostitution, would be a thing of the past.

As Marxist theory concentrated primarily on the relationships of production, the accumulation of capital, and the worker's role in the class struggle, little analysis was given to the relations of reproduction and consumption. Unlike the utopians, Marx did not lay out a detailed description of communist society. How the household would be organized, how the sexes would divide responsibility for housekeeping, who would nurture and socialize children and under what circumstances, Marx and Engels left for future generations of socialists to ponder and decide. As Marxism has become the ideology by which millions of people organize their economic and political system in the twentieth century, it has become clear that a change in the ownership of the means of production does not by itself immediately alter household structure, family ideology, or the relations between the sexes. To do so requires conscious economic, political, cultural, and educational policies which have yet to be devised.

The Kibbutz. Among those involved in the debates over socialism and social reform in the late nineteenth and early twentieth centuries was a group of Eastern European Jews who left Europe to establish the kibbutz movement in Palestine. They were influenced by both the utopians and the Marxists. Like their utopian predecessors in America, the founders of the kibbutz movement had fled to a "new world" to escape religious and economic oppression. Ghettoized, barred from owning land, and subject to sudden persecution in Europe, they now hoped to find a more independent and productive life using their own labor to cultivate their land. Rejecting hierarchical relationships and economic exploitation, the founders of the kibbutz structured their agricultural communities on collective socialist principles. Land was owned by the entire community, labor was shared, and material goods allocated on the basis of "from each according to his ability, to each according to his needs."

The kibbutz leaders, influenced by the first wave of feminist agitation in Europe and America, were committed to equality between the sexes and to the full participation of women in the economic and political sphere. They believed, like Engels, that if women were freed from economic dependence on men, marriages would be held together by love. So they saw to it that each woman was considered as an individual in her economic relations with the collective, not as a wife, daughter, or mother. In addition, kibbutz leaders developed a social structure that would not only free women from economic dependence on men, but would also spare children from control by their biological parents.

Yonina Talmon, an Israeli sociologist who wrote extensively about kibbutz life, pointed out that the founders consciously rejected the requirements of female chastity, lifelong fidelity, and the double standard in male-female relations Their goal in the relationship of women and men was equal partnership in work and love, a voluntary union to be sustained only as long as sincere attachment prevailed.[15]

Today on the kibbutz, when a man and woman decide to live together, they need only apply for a room to have their relationship recognized by the collective. While promiscuity is scorned, the union of a couple does not require legal or religious sanction. Nor does it require extensive or expensive housing. The commune provides the pair with bed-sitting quarters. This is all they need as meals are prepared in a communal kitchen and eaten in a shared dining room. Reading and recreation quarters are also used communally.

When a man and woman decide to live together, or, as they often do, to marry, the woman need change neither her name nor her status. Her husband need never support her, even when she becomes a mother. Women support themselves by their own work, and when they are ill or indisposed, the collective supports them. Likewise, a husband is not dependent on his wife for domestic services because cooking, cleaning, mending, laundry, and other maintenance chores are provided by the community. Having a child poses no economic problems to a young couple, as the kibbutz takes the responsibility for feeding, clothing, and educating all children on an equal basis, regardless of the economic contribution of their mothers and fathers.

Women on the kibbutz continue to work after the birth of children because day-to-day child care is the responsibility of the collective, not of individual parents. From the time of birth, babies live in a nursery under twenty-four-hour supervision by trained nurses. Nurses are female members of the kibbutz, assigned to this job. Babies are visited several times a day by their mothers who come to nurse, and at least once a day by fathers who visit and play. Frequent visits to and from the children's quarters continue throughout childhood. Indeed, kibbutz children spend a great deal of time with their parents. Both parents work close by, and the family is generally together from 4 to 7 P.M.

Although day-to-day, hour-to-hour child care is not the parents' responsibility, biological parents do play an important role in the lives of their children. They serve as special friends and supporters, and as the providers of the long-range loving, intimate connections. They also seem to act as primary role models despite the fact that kibbutz children have many adults and other children with whom they interact. Students of kibbutz life have observed that when parents no longer have the sole responsibility for daily child maintenance, economic support, and discipline, the time spent with offspring is more joyful, and relations between the generations are less strained. As kibbutz children do not have to struggle for independence—having lived away from parents and with peers since birth—family conflicts during adolescence are said to be less intense than in the nuclear household.[16]

The relationship between the adult generation and aging parents is also less irksome and time-consuming on the kibbutz than in noncommunal societies. Adult children visit their aging parents regularly, help with nursing during illness, bring food from communal kitchens when parents are indisposed, and perform a variety of personal services. But the elderly parents' primary economic and physical needs are provided for by the institutions of the collective, so that they retain to the very last

(text continued on page 130)

Alternative Family Patterns

Throughout history, those attempting to create a better society have searched for alternatives to more traditional family structures. Sometimes this has meant modifying existing family forms—for example, retaining the nuclear household as a living unit, but collectivizing housework and child care. In other cases, people have advocated a more thorough transformation of domestic relations, and, like the Oneidans and members of some contemporary communes, have tried to abolish the nuclear family altogether. Frequently, those who build intentional families attempt to provide the opportunity for greater equality between the sexes. Top left: a lesbian couple. Top right: infants in a day-care setting. Bottom: a Shaker community.

a semi-independence. This helps the relationship between the generations to be free of feelings of resentment or guilt often engendered by too-heavy responsibilities.[17]

Kibbutz children are marked by a high devotion to their community and a spirit of cooperation greater than that shown by Israelis raised in the traditional society. The kibbutzniks also constitute a far higher percentage of political and military leaders in Israeli society than their numbers in the population would indicate.

As the founding generation had intended, the kibbutz woman is liberated from economic dependence on one man and from the "double shift" of work in social production and in the home. Kibbutz women do not have to worry about losing their jobs during pregnancy and early child-rearing years. Nor do they have to feel guilty about neglecting their children while they work. Despite these communal supports, observers report that marriage and family are still far more central concerns for kibbutz women than they are for men. Although sexual equality is an articulated value of kibbutz life, women generally do domestic work or child care as their communal jobs. Some women do so-called "male" work, in the field or factory, but few men work at the "female" nurturing jobs.

Israel, a country constantly at the edge of war, lays great stress on military preparedness. This inevitably leads to the idealization of the military man and so-called masculine values such as physical strength, toughness, and bravery. While women do serve in the military, on the kibbutz, as in the rest of the society, men have assumed the most dangerous jobs involving the military defense of the community. These jobs carry with them the highest social esteem. Women are left with the secondary role of providing the emotional and physical support that those engaged in exhausting and nerve-wracking work require.

As collective values have declined in the larger Israeli society, consumer values also have become a greater part of kibbutz life. Families, not individuals, are now acting as units of consumption, with husbands often giving over their own clothing allotments to wives and children to enhance their appearance. Like their counterparts in the traditional society, kibbutz women are taking on the job of managing family purchases.

The plan of the founding generation of kibbutzniks to spread their secular socialist agricultural communities all over Israel has remained a dream. The kibbutz today is a socialist island in a growing urban, consumer society. It is big business in a profit economy. (The kibbutz often employs outside labor, although members still share in the profits.) Israel is also a state ruled by Judaic religious principles with attitudes toward women's role that date back to the days of the Hebrew patriarchs. As the new generation of kibbutzniks absorbs and reflects the economic, religious, and military values that rule the nation, the question arises again, as in the late nineteenth century: Can a socialist, egalitarian, noncompetitive enclave survive in a system stressing competition, individualism, sexism, and consumerism?

The Nuclear Household Transformed

All of the attempts to restructure sexual and family relationships that we have examined so far have been either utopian fantasies, or efforts by small groups that separated themselves from the larger society. Since World War II, profound social and economic changes have been taking place that have done more to alter family ideology and family norms than all the combined efforts of the utopian communitarians in the nineteenth and twentieth centuries. In the last thirty years, women have entered the paid labor force in unprecedented numbers. This phenomenon is taking place both in capitalist and socialist countries. In the United States, women workers support themselves, contribute to family incomes, and facilitate higher levels of consumption. They also create enormous profits for corporations and add to the gross national product.

As the 1980s begin, 45 percent of all women in the United States are full-time workers and 49 percent of the work force is female. Since 1940, the number of married women who hold jobs outside the home has risen fivefold, and married women with preschool children are the fastest-growing category of people entering the paid labor force.[18] Professor Eli Ginzberg, Chairperson of the National Commission on Manpower Policy (sic), described the increasing participation of women in the work force as a revolution that will have a greater impact on society than the rise of communism or the splitting of the atom.[19]

On a worldwide scale, in the last quarter of the twentieth century, 515 million women in both capitalist and socialist nations are working full-time outside the home to meet personal, familial, and national needs. The United Nations estimates that the figure will rise to 600 million by 1980, and that by the year 2000, there will be 842 million women in the world labor force. These changes in women's participation in the labor force have been accompanied by profound alterations in marriage, divorce, child rearing, and household structure. In fact, the nuclear home as norm is being challenged daily, by a variety of other arrangements. As of March 1978, the U.S. Census Bureau reported that one out of every five American households consisted of just one person. The *New York Times* of June 27, 1979, reported that this figure is up a "staggering 42 percent since 1970." The Census study also reports that the number of unmarried couples living together has more than doubled in the period from 1970 to 1978, and that this increase is eightfold among people under twenty-five.

With millions of mothers working full-time outside the home in two-parent households or as single parents, the "double shift" or "double day" for women has become a burden that affects the whole family and the entire society. While communes such as Oneida, almost 150 years ago, and the kibbutz, more recently, succeeded in organizing domestic work and child care in a manner that liberated women from sole responsibility for domestic work and allowed them full participation in the labor force, it is only in the past decade that public policies to deal with the dual-worker family have gained wide attention.

Unlike the founders of Oneida and the kibbutz, some who propose restructuring family and sexual relationships today are, in fact, interested in preserving the nuclear unit, not in dismantling it. They recognize that the nuclear family with two parents working outside the home will not be able to survive as a child-rearing institution if the old sexual division of labor, which assigns women all domestic responsibility, continues. They are attempting, therefore, to develop support systems for the nuclear household and for the mother in the paid labor force and to encourage greater male participation in the domestic sphere. In the United States, such attempts are being made by individuals and private groups of people all over the country. On the whole, though, the government has not yet enacted policies that support the dual-worker family. However, in two small nations, Cuba and Sweden, governments have begun to develop support systems for families with two wage-earning adults. Although at times these programs are insufficient or ineffective, they are significant nonetheless, precisely because they are national policies. Sweden is a social democratic capitalist state with a long tradition of human rights and a high per capita level of production and consumption. Cuba, on the other hand, is a relatively new, underdeveloped socialist country in need of woman's participation in the work force to achieve the higher levels of production and consumption to which it aspires. Both nations have been attempting, within their own historical traditions and economic and political outlooks, to solve the problem of who will take care of the children and how the home will be organized when mothers work full-time outside the home.

The Cuban Family Code. In 1975, Cuba became the first country, capitalist or socialist, to mandate a Family Code that requires men to "cooperate" in housework and child care, even if they are the only members of the family who work outside the home. Clause 26 of the Family Code states that "If one of the spouses contributes only through his or her work in the home and child care, the other spouse must provide full economic support, without this meaning that he or she be relieved of the obligation of cooperation with housework and child care." This clause guarantees the houseworker and the children the economic support necessary for survival. But it does not excuse the worker in the paid labor force from other physical and emotional contributions to domestic maintenance. It is unclear what "cooperating" with housework and child care means in this context, however. It might be reading to the children occasionally or picking up some groceries at the store.

Clause 28 of the Family Code goes even further with the principle of sexual parity by stating that "both spouses have the right to exercise their professions or crafts and must lend each other reciprocal cooperation and aid to this effect." But the code insists that parents will have to organize their home life in such a way as to fulfill their obligations toward their children.

How does the Family Code work in a Latin country with a cultural tradition of "macho" men and passive, domestic women? Dramatic changes do not occur overnight, but those who praise the code claim it is not only a law, but an educational tool as well. Discussion of the proposed legislation stimulated a valuable debate on sex roles and family values in Cuba. Margaret Randall, an American journalist living in Cuba, cites an example. She reports that in a discussion of the Family Code that took place on her block in Havana, an elderly male neighbor said, "You know...I have always believed in helping my wife. We've been married a long time and I cook, clean, and have even taken care of our children and grandchildren. But one thing I never felt right about doing was hanging clothes out on the line. I was afraid people would see me and laugh. Now I guess the time has come to get over these complexes." A woman discussing the new code before its adoption stated, "If they're hoping to incorporate us into the labor force, they're going to have to incorporate themselves into the home."[20]

Attitudes toward male cooperation in the domestic sphere vary with age, as one might expect. Young people in high school see a future in which women will be contributing to society by working outside the home and developing their own potential. They expect cooperation from their husbands and children. In a press conference held on the passage of the Family Code, Vilma Espin, the director of the Federation of Cuban Women, stressed that whether or not wives work or remain inside the home, it is important for *all* men to share household obligations. This will be the only way, she pointed out, that our new generation of children will grow up with a positive image of how men and women should interact.[21] The effectiveness of the Family Code in Cuba will depend partly on women themselves, their demands for cooperation, and their willingness to take their husbands to court for infringements.

The Family Code is only one aspect of Cuba's family policy aimed at integrating women into the work force without disrupting the nuclear family unit. As of 1978 there were close to 650 day-care centers across the island, serving areas with the greatest number of working mothers. More than 54,000 children were educated and cared for in these institutions in 1975. This, however, met the needs of less than 10 percent of the women who needed help to return to the paid labor force. The centers receive infants from the age of forty-five days, the time when paid maternity leave terminates.[22] As the economy cannot yet support a sufficient number of infant centers (*circulos*) to accommodate all children, priority is given to the children of mothers who work outside the home. Some employed women have mothers, fathers, grandmothers, and grandfathers to call upon for help with child care, as the extended family household remains strong in Cuba. Married couples, as well as single and divorced adults, often live with their parents due to the housing shortage. The tradition of one man and one woman living in a nuclear home and being solely responsible for all aspects of child rearing is not as strong in Cuba as it is among urban middle-class families in the United States. In Cuba, as among Native Americans, Hispanics, and blacks, the tradition has been for extended networks of generations of women to cooperate in child-rearing responsibilities. However, in Cuba, this network is becoming increasingly involved in the paid labor force, making it imperative that the day-care system be expanded.

Other social services for the dual-worker family have been developed in the twenty years since the Cuban revolution. Almost all workplaces either have their own dining rooms or give workers access to dining rooms at nearby factories. Grade school children have hot lunch programs, and beginning with junior high school, a large percentage of children take advantage of the boarding school system. In boarding schools throughout the country, children live and study all week, returning to their families only for weekends.

In addition to the household arrangements in the nuclear unit, Cuba's Family Code covers divorce and responsibility for children. In line with its commitment to new relationships of equality between the sexes, child support is not automatically expected of the man. In a case where the woman is working for pay and the man is studying, it might be the responsibility of the woman. Custody of children is not automatically given to the woman in a divorce case.

Cuba has spent the past twenty years constructing a new set of economic and political relations. The government is also in the process of redefining family relations and the meaning of motherhood and fatherhood in ways that depart from the centuries-old tradition of male supremacy. The government, however, continues to view the heterosexual nuclear family as the basic cell of society. In the past, Cuba has taken harsh measures to punish homosexual relationships, which it views as "counterrevolutionary." In recent years, however, official hostility toward homosexuals has become more muted.

Cuba is a young nation. It may not be able to immediately transform traditional family and sex roles. But its national policy recognizes that the success of the Family Code is linked organically to a program for sexual parity in the workplace and eventually in the political sphere. Cuba is promising women, men, and children more options within the nuclear unit than the former system allowed. Whether it will fulfill its promise is of great interest to all those who study families and who live in them.

Family Policy in Sweden. The need to provide young children with good physical and psychological care, while at the same time easing the burden of parenthood for gainfully employed men and women living in the nuclear household, has become a central political issue in Sweden in the past decade. Those responsible for family policy and social welfare recognize that children are born with a need for nurturance, intimacy, security, and continuity of care. Dr. Bror Rexed, Director General of Sweden's National Board of Health and Welfare, noted in May 1976 that although working parents want to give children as much love and stimulation as possible, they are too fatigued to do so after they have worked all day, journeyed home from work, and completed their housekeeping chores. When "fatigue weighs down every limb and the head feels washed out," he added, "all parents can do is put their children to bed."[23]

Camilla Odhnoff, a former cabinet minister for family policy and in 1975 chairperson of the Commission on Family Assistance, reported that those planning family policy in Sweden believe that "it is absurd to build a society on the two-income breadwinning principle unless that society does something in return to give parents reasonable opportunities to combine work with family life."[24]

Family policy in Sweden today emphasizes shared parenting, according to a 1975 report by the Prime Minister's Advisory Council on Equality Between Men and Women. "Fathers are now accorded the same degree of responsibility and importance in the children's lives as has always been accorded to mothers."[25] Solutions to the questions, who shall take care of the children, and how, are being sought in three areas: (1) the expansion of public child-care facilities; (2) the provision of more work-free time for parents of small children; (3) gender-role and parenting education to counteract sex-role stereotypes.

In 1969, Sweden instituted a national program for sex-role education. It required that information on gender stereotypes, career options for women as well as men, and instruction on the responsibilities and the techniques of child care be given to both sexes at all stages of the educational process. Today, the official curricula of both elementary and secondary schools assume that "men and women will play the same role in the future... preparation for the parental role is just as important for boys as for girls, and that girls have reason to be just as interested in their careers as boys."[26]

The spring 1979 session of parliament approved a bill that makes available voluntary parental training during paid working hours for the fathers and mothers of newborn infants. The fathers of newborn babies will, under this program, be invited to the hospital maternity ward for a day to become acquainted with the baby and learn to take care of it. In addition, a series of ten to twelve classes conducted before childbirth and an equal number afterward are offered during paid working hours for both parents. These classes, led by child-care experts, examine the problems, pleasures, and techniques of parenthood.[27]

In recent years in Sweden, about 6,000 fathers a year have

taken leave from their jobs for one month or longer to take care of their newborn infants while mothers are at work. This is made possible by a parental insurance system introduced in 1974, which entitles one parent at a time to stay home with a newborn baby while receiving 90 percent of full pay. The parental insurance system is financed by an 85 percent contribution from employers and a 15 percent contribution from the central government. Parents may divide their paid leave between them, or one parent may use it all. A third alternative is for both parents to work half-time (and receive 90 percent of their pay) if that can be arranged. A new ruling also allows parents to reserve the final three months of the nine-month paid leave period to use bit by bit until their child reaches age eight. Additional opportunities for leave were instituted on January 1, 1979. From that date on, all parents are granted the legal right to a six-hour work day during a child's first eight years or a full leave of absence for eighteen months. But there is no compensation for these leaves beyond the nine-month period. The Social Democrats, now out of office, oppose the unpaid leave provisions on the grounds that they will be used mainly by women, thus weakening women's chances for competing in the labor market. They also argue that those taking unpaid leaves will be women with well-paid husbands, while poor women or single mothers will not benefit at all.

As a rule, the fathers who have taken advantage of parental leave have done so after the mother has been at home breastfeeding the baby for a few months. Those men who have taken the opportunity to participate in infant care—about 10 to 12 percent of those eligible—have been concentrated in the intellectual professions and in families where wives also have a good income. Few applications for paternity leave have come from industrial workers. But one area where fathers seem to be taking advantage of the paid leave is in the sixty-day annual leave to care for a sick child. Fathers are reported to take more advantage of this leave benefit than any other aspect of parental insurance. A 1975 report to the prime minister indicated that 30 to 40 percent of fathers use this benefit when a child under ten falls ill, or when a new child is born and there is no one at home to look after the older children. Sheila Kamerman points out in a survey on work and family in industrialized society that even if men use the leave benefit less than women, its availability for men diminishes the possibilities of discrimination against women.[28]

While the expansion of public child care is an important aspect of Swedish family policy, a shortage of facilities still exists. Day care is provided in three different types of programs. The most widespread is the day-care center, open from 7:00 A.M. until 6:30 P.M. for children aged three to seven. (Seven is the age Swedish children enter the public schools.) An after-school recreational program provides day care for school-age children until parents return from work. For children under three, the "family day care" program provides a "day mother" who is paid a salary by the government to take care of several children in her own home. All three types of facilities are in short supply in Sweden, however. The total of 221,000 openings for preschool children, for example, should be seen in relationship to the 450,000 preschool children in the country whose mothers work full-time or part-time. In 1976, parliament approved a program for creating 100,000 new places in day-care centers and 50,000 new openings in after-school programs, but there are doubts whether municipalities will fulfill their quotas.[29]

Many employed mothers would like to see public day care organized on a twenty-four-hour basis. A survey conducted in the early 1970s found that 57 percent of women factory workers and 69 percent of women in white-collar employment would like some form of round-the-clock municipal day care. But Swedish child-care planners feel that although small children benefit greatly from group care in terms of intellectual stimulation and emotional growth, they should spend a significant portion of their day in intimate relations within the home.[30] That is why family policy planners are stressing the parental leave program and the six-hour day.

Widespread discussion of the child-parent relationship in Sweden may be viewed as one aspect of the national effort to restructure the traditional family. Polls have been taken of Swedish children to find out what they talk about to one another and what they ask themselves about a variety of life problems. Much to the surprise of members of the national boards of health and welfare, children often think about sharing responsibility and looking out for one another. Fairly often they feel lonely and forlorn. They wonder about why their elders live as they do, and why adults work so hard. They also wonder why they were brought into this world, and what is to become of them.

These problems confront children in most industrial societies in which the places for production are separated from the household. Concerned child psychologists and welfare workers in Sweden propose that children be integrated into the adult job world at an early age. Visits to parents' place of work, the creation of day-care centers connected to the workplace, and early admission to the job market for teenagers are suggested to counter the alienation between parents and children.[31] The physical and mental environment of children and the quality of their contacts with parents and other adults are significant issues in Sweden's industrialized society, debated hotly by political parties in national elections.

In a book entitled *A Child's Right to Divorce*, published in 1978, Ulla Jacobson, a professor of law at the University of Stockholm, proposed that a child should have the right to divorce its parents. Legislation to that affect has already been introduced in parliament, but not enacted as yet. Jacobson argues that "parents and children can be poorly suited to each other without anyone being to blame."[32] It should be possible to regard the child's right to divorce not as a chance for the child to accuse the parents, but as an entirely reasonable expedient in a poor relationship. Of course, there are economic and legal problems to be worked out should a child's right to divorce become law. Jacobson contends that inheritance rights and maintenance obligations have been, and are still, tied directly to biological parenthood and need not be affected by granting children the right to divorce.[33] But we have seen from our study of the family that property and ownership, economic support and dominance, are usually intertwined.

Despite the continuing expansion of day care, parental leave, and sex-role education, there are still few substantial changes in the sexual division of labor in Sweden or in household organization. Surveys of working-class families where both partners work in the paid labor force still find the wife chiefly responsible for the care of the children and the housework. Rita Liljestrom, a prominent Swedish sociologist concerned with family policy, attributes male reluctance to devote more attention to the home and to child rearing to the fact that men regard themselves primarily as breadwinners. Work takes so much out of them that they have virtually nothing left to give their families. They see home as a place for recovery and rest, while women see home as a place of work.[34]

These attitudes are partly due to the fact that most women are still marginal earners compared with men. They are concentrated in unskilled work and in low-paying professions. The Prime Minister's Advisory Council on Equality Between Men and Women noted this problem in 1975. "In spite of pay equalization between the sexes, great differences remain, above all because women and men work in different occupations."[35] Only if women can hold the same types of jobs as men on all levels of skill and training and receive equal pay for similar work, will men begin to work in the home on an equal basis with women. Equality between the sexes in the family depends on people's ability to integrate private and public roles, reproductive and productive roles.

Sweden accepts the nuclear family as the unit of social reproduction and is making every effort to support it at a time when women's role in the labor force is becoming increasingly important. This support for the nuclear unit can change the organizational structure and the ideology of the family in the years to come. A careful study of Swedish family policies promises important insights for Americans, who have yet to evolve any coherent program to meet the problems of the dual-worker family and the relations between parents and children in an industrialized consumer society.

Shared Parenting in the United States. In the United States, the government has not yet officially recognized the economic cost of parenting, nor its social value. It has yet to develop policies to support the nuclear family with two employed parents. As more and more mothers enter the work force, individuals and couples have had to devise their own ways of dealing with the "double burden" of work inside and outside the home. Many have come to recognize that "mothering" is not necessarily a sex-linked capacity and that shared parenting can be rewarding for children, for fathers, for mothers, and for society.

For at least a decade, some fathers have been participating in the actual birth of daughters and sons. Denying that birthing is only women's work, they find that their presence and involvement in labor and delivery results in stronger and more immediate bonding with their offspring. Newspaper stories, television talk shows, and the glossy magazines have also begun to report a variety of "novel" child-care arrangements that couples and single parents are making. In a provocative book, *Who Will Raise the Children: New Options for Fathers,* James A. Levine presents a variety of alternatives within the private household that allow fathers to share in child care or to take over the complete responsibility while mothers work in the paid labor force.[36] A businessman and an artist, for instance, have developed a pattern of joint housework and care for their preschool child. The husband began to feel that his drive for success in business was keeping him away from the newborn baby. Eric, as the man is called in the case history Levine presents, realized that he did not want to have the same distant relationship with his son that he had had with his own father, who was always away on business. Eric decided it would be better to work part-time at his job and remain at home part-time. Fortunately, his proposal was agreeable to his employers, who realized, as some employers do, that they can get more than half-time work from half-time workers.

Eric undertook the responsibility for two-fifths of the child care and housework, while he assumed three-fifths of the household's financial burden. This meant that Pam, the wife and mother, would take care of the child and house three-fifths of the time and pay only two-fifths of the expenses. This unequal division of economic and household responsibilities took place because the man's earning capacity was considerably greater than the woman's—which is not unusual. On weekends, the parents shared all domestic chores and responsibilities on a fifty-fifty basis. When Eric was on duty, he cooked, bathed, and entertained his son, while Pam worked in her home office. He cleaned the kitchen and the rest of the house, took his son out in the baby carriage, shopped, and did the laundry. Eric found that he became more aware of the amount of work that goes into keeping house and taking care of a child. Even on the days that Eric worked at the office, Pam did not have to feel frantic about getting a perfect dinner on the table or having her son quietly tucked into bed. Eric was more willing to help on his "off-duty" hours because he understood the amount of labor and time that goes into every aspect of child care. Men who take care of children in the private nuclear household report that they experience the same loneliness, frustration, and fatigue as women, even when they know that the job is only part-time and could be temporary if they chose to make it so.

For some parents, the best way to combine paid work and domestic work is through sharing the same full-time paid job. According to a study made by an independent employment research institute, most job sharing on record is being done by female teams, but a growing number of married couples are beginning to take advantage of this new version of "flex-time." In January 1980, the *New York Times* reported on a recent study done by the National Council for Alternative Work Patterns. The study listed twenty-eight U.S. corporations, institutions, or agencies—including the states of Maryland and Oregon—that have embraced job sharing. Alternative work patterns, according to the study, provide "tangible economic benefits to the employer," and also "enable employees to mesh job demands with their personal and family needs."[37]

At Earlham College in Indiana, one husband and wife share a full professorship and its salary, while dividing equally the housework and child care responsibilities. "We have found this to be a really good way to organize our lives," Alice Shrock told a United Press International reporter. "I teach during the fall and winter semesters and Alice teaches during the winter and spring so one of us is home all the time," Randall Shrock explained.

"During the winter we hire a student to help with the housework." The Shrocks, like a growing number of other academic couples, feel that the plan is working well because it allows them to balance their professional and private lives. In the long run, they feel that their daughter will be the greatest beneficiary. Not only will she have a closer involvement with her father than the old division of labor allows, but she will also have a much less constricted view of sex roles. The Shrocks hope that seeing a mother and father trade off domestic and professional jobs will give their daughter a broader sense of the options and possibilities available to her as a woman.[38]

Another couple shares a position at Hampshire College in Massachusetts. They divide their time roughly into two daily blocks, nine-to-one and one-to-five. One works at home and one at school in this time frame. Kurt, the father, found the experience of caring for his first child so exciting that he decided to continue the arrangement when the second child was born. He explains, "I am refreshed when I am at home with the children and I am refreshed when I'm teaching at the college. And there is a terrific side benefit to sharing. We have so much better communication as a family. . . . I think our marriage is much stronger for this sharing." Child care and housework are not all pleasure, however, as Kurt realized when he began to stay home. One semester when both children were still very little, his schedule worked out so that he had to spend one and a half days straight with the children. "Was I ever ready to go to college!" he reported. In this case, each parent has been offered a full-time job elsewhere, but neither wants to give up the time spent at home with their two children.[39]

A unique arrangement in child sharing was initiated by the Lesbian Community Center in Baltimore in 1975. Members of the center believed that "true community does not come from only one group coming together." Women who are not mothers, they suggested, could give support to lesbian mothers by sharing with them some of the responsibilities of child care. They noted that lesbians may be estranged not only from the fathers of their children, but from their families of origin as well. Lacking the aunts, uncles, cousins, and grandparents who can lend support, they may also fear asking social service agencies for help because they might be declared unfit as mothers. The non-mothers who initiated the child-sharing idea saw it as a way to relate to children without having children of their own. They saw their project as more than a baby-sitting service. They wished to develop long-term relationships of support and companionship with the children, thus giving the children additional adults with whom to interact. They also hoped that by giving the mothers free time for themselves, relations between the mothers and children would be improved.[40]

So far intentional shared parenting seems to be the privilege of professionals, highly skilled executives, or the self-employed who can structure their work schedules to suit their needs. However, there has always been a large group of parents who shared child care through necessity. Driven by poverty, and with no one to rely on but themselves, mothers have worked the night shift so that they could be at home during the day with their children. Likewise, fathers have worked at night so that they could be at home while mothers worked during the day. Unfortunately, there is usually little joy in these arrangements, as fatigue, the parents' need for free time, and societal designation of housework as a female job rob both children and adults of relaxed and joyful contact.

For shared parenting to work for more than a tiny number of middle-class families, substantial changes in the organization of the work force, in governmental policies toward the family and child care, and in attitudes toward parenting are necessary. Some of these changes, mainly in attitudes toward parenting, are beginning to take place. Dr. Benjamin Spock, whose best-selling book, *Baby and Child Care*, influenced parents in the 1940s, '50s, and '60s, formerly advised fathers to change diapers only occasionally. He cautioned that forcing men who abhorred participating in baby care to do so could be counterproductive. Dr. Spock assumed, in his early writings, that mothers would and should be available at home. The father's educational and socializing role with his children was connected to his life in the paid work force and the community outside the home. For this attitude, Dr. Spock earned a good deal of criticism from the women's movement in the 1970s. He reevaluated his ideas and revised his book in 1976 "to eliminate the sexist biases of the sort that help to create and perpetuate discrimination against girls and women."[41] His 1976 edition of *Baby and Child Care* now concludes, "A father with a full-time job—even where a mother is staying at home—will do best by his children, his wife and himself if he takes half or more of the management of children and also participates in the housework." Spock then goes on to tell the thousands of parents who still read his books that

It will be a great day when fathers . . . consider the care of their children to be as important to *them* as their jobs and careers . . . seek out jobs and work schedules that will allow them ample time to be with their wives and children . . . [and] will let it be known at their workplaces that they take their parental responsibilities very seriously and may have to take time off when their children need them just as working mothers have always done.[42]

Contemporary Communal Families

Many people who are dissatisfied with family life accept the nuclear household as the basic unit for intimate relations and for child rearing. They merely wish to improve its functioning in an industrial, consumer society where mothers work as well as fathers, and where greater equality between the sexes is becoming an accepted goal. Some, however, do not wish to retain the nuclear family. They believe that communal or collective living is an attractive alternative to the isolation of the nuclear family. Group living can sometimes offer a practical and humane way to manage the double burden of paid work and child rearing. For some, it is seen as an antidote to the wastefulness, individualism, and emotional deprivation they experienced within the nuclear household.

Many of those who advocate communal living are middle-class young adults who were raised in small towns and suburbs where houses are as far apart as one can afford, where gainful employment is a long distance off, and where fathers work too hard in order to support the household to spend much time in it.

In the middle-class family, where privacy and self-sufficiency are stressed as positive values, contact with kinfolk and with the older generation may be minimal and children are likely to be primarily engaged with one adult, usually the mother. Children raised in middle-class households often have no contact with or knowledge of productive labor. Some report that, as they were growing up, they had no notion of what their fathers actually did all day. To combat this arrid, lonely atmosphere which sometimes leads to tranquilizers and alcohol for mothers and depression for children, thousands of young adults in the past two decades have turned to experiments in communal living for themselves and their children. They have been joined by some middle-aged and older people who also find group living more appealing than the isolation of the nuclear household.

It was the threat of social isolation in her adult life that prompted one woman to join an urban commune. She was married to a long-distance truck driver and had no kin nearby. She dreaded the days and nights when her husband would be on the road and she would be confined to the house, caring for a newborn infant alone. In the commune, she hoped to find other adult companionship and people who would help care for the baby while she left home for errands or recreation. Her husband, on the other hand, was reluctant to give up the pleasure and intimacy of returning to a private household after a long trip. He finally agreed to join the commune on the promise that their lives would be richer for the variety of companions and opportunities for emotional growth offered by collective living.[43]

Communal living can be a lifeline for the single parent who must cope alone with all the demands of a job and children. "Raising a child alone is not easy," Larraine Skinner explained to a reporter from the New York Times recently. Ms. Skinner, a secretary, and her eleven-year-old daughter, Laurie, had been living alone. They decided that they could make their lives a little more secure by moving in with Judy Agins and her eight-year-old daughter Jennifer. The Skinners, a black family, and the Agins, who are Jewish, call their new household "our interracial commune." The Skinner-Agins household pools its rent money and shares the cooking, cleaning, and child-care responsibilities. All household members feel that they live a lot better now. "When it's one-on-one, twenty-four hours a day, you go crazy," said Ms. Agins, a voice teacher. Now both mothers have company and diversions, and so do the children.[44] With their own parents and siblings often living far away, a growing number of single parents are beginning to form communal households. Some couples, too, are finding that they need help in child rearing and a broader circle of emotional contacts than the nuclear household provides.

Many kinds of communal living arrangements are being tried in both urban and rural areas. Communes vary a great deal with regard to how they carry out certain essential domestic tasks, including child rearing, cooking, and housework. The amount of privacy an individual or couple has varies, as do sexual norms. Many factors shape particular communes, including age of members, geographic location, kind of paid work that sustains members, and political ideals of those who live in the commune. One way to look at communes is to divide them into two very large categories. One, which we will call the circle of families, rejects the nuclear household as a living unit but builds on the relationships of that unit. The other, the counterculture or anarchistic commune, rejects nuclear family relationships as well as private living arrangements. While these categories can help us to understand the nature of communes, they are not absolute distinctions. Many communes fall somewhere in between the two categories and take features from both.

The Circle of Families. For those who find the nuclear unit burdensome and emotionally unfulfilling, but who are still committed to monogamous sexual relations and private parent-hood, the circle of families offers an alternative. The circle of families is a residential collective in which the nuclear unit is the essential component. Some circles of families include single adults without children, but child rearing, to which all must contribute, is an essential feature of this form of communal life. In a circle of families, each nuclear unit usually has its own sleeping and study quarters and a private space where they can be alone together when they feel the need. Sitting rooms, play areas, cooking and dining facilities, are generally shared by the entire collective. Adults share expenses and tasks within the domestic sphere, and children also contribute to household maintenance according to their capacities.

While any set of parents is free to make its own decision regarding the educational and social values by which its own children are raised, communal decisions and interaction are highly valued. The people who decide to live together in a circle of families usually make this decision not only because they find the private nuclear unit too burdensome, but also because they believe in community and cooperation as life-enhancing values. They reject the excessive consumerism and competition that is involved in "keeping up with the Joneses," and want to present their children with a model of society that abolishes constant references to "mine and thine."

Companionship with other adults is another important motivation in family communes. A woman living in a two-family circle in a suburban community commented that the most immediate joy of communal living was companionship during the day. Shared household chores and talking away frustration with another woman made life easier. In addition:

For me, living communally makes it possible to enjoy the companionship of men other than my husband easily and naturally as individuals and friends.... Outside a commune I wouldn't have the opportunity to discuss books or play the guitar or just have some good conversation with male friends on the evenings when Dave is busy or not at home. Dave and I realize how these things have enriched us, how lopsided our lives would be if we had continued to limit our friendships outside our marriage to "the girls" for me and "the guys" for him.[45]

Some of the contemporary circles of families that have been studied by sociologists or reported on in the media are interested in abolishing traditional sex roles. In most of these communes, both men and women work outside and inside the home. The division of labor within the home takes different forms in different circles, but equality and rotation of chores are the most common principles. It is generally easier for adults to participate in all communal functions if they have some flexibility in their outside work schedules. This kind of flexibility is more available to the self-employed, the professional, the artist, or the student than it is to the industrial worker. This is probably one of many reasons why most circles of families that have been studied and described consist of middle-class people.

In one circle of families located in Brooklyn, New York, four adults split a twelve-hour day into four three-hour housework duty shifts. Each adult works three hours and gets nine hours free. All adults share laundry, cooking, shopping, and child care on an equal basis. In Philadelphia, a circle of families arranges work and responsibility in another way. The Philadelphia Life Center, which in 1973 consisted of thirteen houses inhabited by 100 adults and children, is a circle of families that also accommodates single people. They include parents and nonparents, and they range in age from young adults in their twenties to older people in their sixties. An interview with the Lakeys, who live in a unit of the Philadelphia Life Center, describes life with three other nonrelated persons in an extended family setting.[46] In each of the communal houses, all housekeeping and child care are borne equally by men as well as women. The Lakeys reported that they share roles in almost every aspect of their marriage. George assumes responsibility for the children at least two days a week. When he is traveling in his capacity as an organizer for the American Friends Service Committee, Berit is required to give more time to child care. But this is not overwhelming, as she shares this added responsibility with the three other adults at home.

Tensions develop in the circle of families, just as they do in the nuclear home. According to the ideology in the nuclear unit, particularly as portrayed on television or in the glossy magazines, conflict among family members is viewed as a sign of failure or a lack of love. In an intentional community, however, conflict is anticipated and the process of resolving difficulties is considered a creative and essential element of human growth. In communal living, attempts to evolve equal and nonoppressive relations, and the pressures created by a certain lack of privacy, require deliberate attention. Discussion sessions in which private feelings of anger are expressed, and where not only criticism but care and concern are offered, are considered by many communards to be among the most rewarding aspects of communal life.

Men in the Philadelphia Life Center created a discussion group to deal with the discomfort some of them felt about their new domestic and nurturing responsibilities. They examined questions such as "What does it really mean to be a man?" and "How have we been brought up to view the male role?" George Lakey reported that the discussion group helped him realize that he does not have to live up to the image of a movie-star or sports hero. He says he can now cry when he feels like it, thus releasing pent-up anger and allowing tenderness to emerge.

Circles of families recognize the close and primary bonds of monogamous couples and of parents and children. Their purpose is not to challenge these intimate relationships, but to enhance the joyful aspects of family life. They try to lighten economic, physical, and psychological burdens by extending support systems beyond the nuclear unit. By collectivizing domestic chores, family communes relieve women of the primary responsibility for the home and children. This affords women greater opportunities for paid work, education, recreation, and community activities. Communal life also reduces the power of men over women in that decisions are made collectively, with women and men sharing in the process. This changes the nature of a woman's relationship to her husband and children, thus giving her greater self-esteem, not only at home, but on the job and in the community.

Counterculture Communes. Some contemporary communes attempt to do away with the nuclear unit altogether. Their members generally recognize neither monogamous marriage nor exclusive parental control over children. Their search is for individual freedom and fulfillment on the one hand, and an extended community of love and support on the other. In most counterculture communes, members have chosen to separate themselves from the larger society because they wish to free themselves from all forms of hierarchy, authority, sexual domination, coercion, and competition. They condemn ecological waste, pollution of the atmosphere, excessive consumerism, social conformity, and production for profit. Because these communes reject the dominant values and behavior patterns of society, they have been labeled "counterculture" by sociologists and journalists. Bennet Berger, Bruce M. Hacket and R. Mervyn Miller, who studied thirty-eight counterculture communes (also known as hippie and anarchist communes) in the early 1970s, found that most communards were seeking such traditional family values as love, support, acceptance, a sense of place, and a model for child rearing. Most commune members like to think of themselves as part of an extended family of peers, sometimes even adopting the same surname or, in one instance, calling themselves "The Family." A variety of living arrangements coexist in these communities, including monogamous nuclear units and unmarried couples, both heterosexual and homosexual. In addition, there are individual women and men moving in and out of relationships. Berger et al. characterize these relationships as "serial monogamy." They point out that although celibacy is rare and relations between couples can be fragile, this does not mean that "sex is either promiscuous or disordered."[47] Communities that practice group marriage are very much the exception. They are usually beset with so many interpersonal problems that few survive as long as one year. This makes it hard to develop a significant study of their patterns of organization and interaction.

The need for an intentional family can be particularly compelling for lesbian women, who may be estranged from their kin and the larger society. To fill their need for a loving and supportive environment, a number of women's communes, both rural and urban, have been organized. One such is the "Community," which has been functioning as an extended network of choice in Portland, Oregon, for a number of years. The Community provides its members with a place to live in one of a number of dwellings scattered throughout the city, and also provides gainful employment in such commune-run enterprises as a gas station, a child-care center, a health clinic, a bookstore, and a house-painting business. There are three requirements for

membership in the Community: identifying with the counterculture youth movement and advocating its ideals; devoting the
major portion of one's time and energy to Community affairs,
including recreational, cultural, and political activities; and
placing a primary value on being a lesbian.

Members of the Community devote virtually all their time
and energy to communal activities of work, play, and interpersonal relationships. Ex-lovers are expected to remain friends
in the Community. Those who cannot do this are asked to leave.
A group of anthropologists from Portland State University who
studied the Community examined personal and group relationships. They contend that members eventually consent to give
their personal pair relationships secondary status because they
believe that the support, acceptance, and companionship the
group offers are more stable and enduring than what pair relations
can provide.[48]

A woman in another commune, the Womanshare Collective, a
rural farm commune in Grants Pass, Oregon, explains what
collective living means to her.

Collectivity is my chosen way to change and grow.... I live here with
these four women because I need a "home." I need a connection with a
group beyond myself, and a connection with the earth that endures. We
may not always be the same five women. We may not always live on this
land. But I know that I must be with the women and that we must be
connected to the earth. Now I am no longer alone. I am part of the
collective *we*, and we endure.[49]

Child rearing

Child rearing is one of the difficult problems that has yet to be
resolved in many contemporary American communes. Conflicts
arise over differing levels of commitment to children and over
contradictory ideas about the proper care and education of
children. Children are given a great deal of freedom in most
counterculture communes. Until the age of four they seem to be
in the care of their mothers, but after that they are considered to
be persons in their own right. They generally become full-fledged
members of the commune, entitled to attend meetings and to
make their feelings, desires, and criticisms known.[50] In some
communities, they may even participate in decision making.

Along with these responsibilities often go the general "adult" privileges of the commune, for example, choosing whether or when one wants to work, study, or watch television.[51] It is assumed that after the age of four, children are capable of doing things for themselves, so parents and other adults may refuse to fetch and tote for them. Further, they are considered old enough to do something useful for others and are frequently asked to do light chores and run errands. In rural communes engaged in agriculture or other forms of productive labor, small children may observe and participate on their own level. As parents are not judged by their children's transgressions or accomplishments, child-parent relations can become quite relaxed.

On the other hand, the philosophy of "doing one's own thing" can boomerang for children. Jessie Bernard, a sociologist specializing in family relations, has found that when adults are encouraged to come and go as the spirit moves them, children find that they cannot count on continuous and permanent intimate relations. This can leave them feeling lonely and isolated.[52] In an autobiographical report of a year in the life of a city commune, Michael Weiss tells the following story about his eight-year-old son, Matt:

"Are Gary and Anne leaving the house?" he asked, between sobs. Oh god, Ruth [his mother] thought, eight years old, why does he have to go through this? "Probably they will be next summer," she said, stroking his hair.

"It's just like last year with Gil and Wendy," he said, during a pause while he tried to catch his breath. "Communal living...just isn't worth it...if...everybody keeps going away."

"Yes," Ruth said, "yes, baby, I feel that way too." She wanted to protect him from sadness, and here she had put him in the middle of an ever-changing grown-up world. Shouldn't a kid feel that there are people he can depend on absolutely?[53]

Questions of how much control parents should have over their children continue to be debated in counterculture communes. Berger reports that infants and "knee babies" are almost universally in the charge of their mothers, who have primary responsibility for their care. Members of some communes have discussed the possibility of "communalizing" infants, placing them at any available breast rather than exclusively at the mother's. But this is still considered too radical, although it was proposed by Plato more than two thousand years ago. In some communes, mothers complain of feeling abandoned when other commune members leave or do not fulfill their responsibilities for child-rearing tasks. When others take over in times of stress, mothers and fathers report that they feel guilty and wonder whether they are good parents.

Some contemporary communes are making special efforts to deal with these issues. Rainbow Community is particularly committed to nonauthoritarian and caring child rearing. The commune is part of the Movement for a New Society, an organization committed to a nonviolent transition to socialism. Rainbow Community is composed of Fai and Sandra, two single parents; Alan, Adam, Steve, and Firefly, who are single men; and four children, Julie, Aaron, Nathan, and Kyle. The adults range in age from twenty-four to thirty-seven years; the children, from six to ten. This commune requires its members to have a "strong commitment to nurture children, as something adults value for their own growth (not just as a maintenance task); and to see relating to children as revolutionary involvement."[54]

In addition to sharing tasks and resources, the Rainbow Community has worked out a careful and constantly evolving plan for child care. Weekly, each adult is with the children two mornings, from rising time until they leave for school; one afternoon, from 3:30 to supper; and one evening. There is also one block of time set aside to be with the children during the weekend. Child-care times require that the adult's attention be committed solely to the children. This does not mean that they do everything for them. Adult members act on the principle that children should do everything they can for themselves. Children at Rainbow Community prepare all of their own meals and clean up after themselves. Even Kyle, at the age of six, can scramble or fry an egg, flip a pancake, and make puddings.

The adults in Rainbow Community feel that when they were young, they lacked support in working through hurts and conflicts with other children, and they rarely received recognition for courage or creativity. They are attempting to provide what they missed to the children in their care. All the adults in the commune make dates with individual children about once a month for movies, bowling, ice skating, cards, playing pool, or going out to eat. Bedtime is also special-treat time. The adults find that when you have to spend only one evening a week doing it, it's fun. After cards, popcorn, or talking, the big event is "the story." Bedtime stories have become great opportunities for sharing ideas and values with children.

For the members of Rainbow Community, children's libera-tion is a specific way of building a new society. The adults claim that they are learning to empower children to take responsibility for meeting their own needs. They believe that children are oppressed when parents withhold opportunities for taking responsibility, ignore children, or put them down verbally.

Feminism is another primary commitment of all adults in the commune. This affects their process of child rearing. Members try to be aware of sexist language and "how loud and dominating men's voices can be." They also are aware of how choices of household tasks either support or counteract traditional expectations of male and female roles.

Although all the adults in Rainbow Community are highly involved with each other, there are no primary sexual relation-ships among them. If two members should desire such a relationship, they have to leave the commune. Like the Oneidans, the members of Rainbow Community believe that exclusive relationships between couples weaken the cohesive feeling of the whole.

As members of the Rainbow Community have found, sharing in child rearing can be a life-enhancing experience for women and men who have chosen not to become biological parents, as well as for biological parents. A male commune member shared these feelings in an essay in *Communities,* a journal of cooperative living:

As a person who made a conscious decision not to reproduce, I realized that I had a lot of love and nurturance to offer and no place to go with that.... I enjoy this opportunity to share in fixing breakfasts, looking for shoes, and explaining that I am not "daddy" but I really love them and will still be here next year too. Sure I've opened myself up to new feelings—like learning how to let go of them so they can dream and wander and go and grow.[55]

The Future for All of Us

Throughout history, people have dreamed of and developed intentional alternatives to the traditional family of their time. Most of these have been attempts to improve the biological family's ability to function in times of changing political and cultural expectations. In the nineteenth century, there were those like Melusina Fay Peirce and Charlotte Perkins Gilman who wished to collectivize housework because they found it oppressive and wasteful when performed by the individual housewife in her isolated home. These feminists retained the nuclear family as the basic unit of living, loving, and child rearing. But they wished to make it a more satisfying, less confining place for women. Today their feminist counterparts are attempting to build egalitarian marriages through female-male sharing of child care, domestic work, and financial support of the home. They are trying to bring the family into harmony with the demands and values of present day life. In Cuba and Sweden, national governments are attempting to alter a traditional division of labor within the household and provide the nuclear unit with the support it needs for child rearing. Their purpose is to preserve the nuclear family structure by modifying it.

From Plato to the Oneidans to members of contemporary communes, there have been, throughout history, those who have advocated a more thorough transformation of domestic relations. They have worked to abolish the nuclear family as the center of relations of love and dependence between the sexes and generations. Often even those who discard monogamous marriage and parental control—such as counterculture communards—see their way of life as familial. They are seeking a bigger, better, and happier family than the one they came from. Although such radical alternatives are usually envisioned by only a small segment of the population, they are of interest to large numbers of people seeking to understand the dynamics of family life.

While literary utopias allow our imagination to soar and are based on improbable combinations and relationships, intentional communities are more realistic social laboratories. There, ideas concerning domestic arrangements can be tested with real human beings, even if they live in isolation from the larger society. Examining communal experiments, their successes and failures, illuminates ways to organize contemporary families. It also helps one understand the difficulties inherent in attempts to develop family policies that can serve the needs of young and old, female and male, those who desire absolute freedom and those who seek permanent commitment. Attempts to build alternative communities such as Frances Wright's Nashoba, the kibbutz, or an anarchist commune also illustrate the problems involved in developing new structures in a culture and economic system not receptive to such changes.

The search for alternatives to traditional family forms underlines the way in which the family interacts with the economic, political, and cultural institutions and shows how difficult it is for one family or one community to sustain unconventional arrangements. Sharing domestic work and economic support equally within a family remains a utopian dream for most Americans when women earn, on the average, 60 percent of what men earn. Although job sharing may be an attractive option for middle-class couples who work in relatively high-paying professions, many families cannot survive sharing one low income. The cooperative households examined in this book have been composed of men and women who generally work flexible hours. This is not possible for most workers today. Communes that have dissolved due to competition, jealousy, and economic chaos make it clear that in a society that values and rewards individualism, competition, and material wealth, living collectively will probably be uncomfortable for the majority of people.

But in these alternative models of the past and present, we can also find hope for the future. They help to clarify the kinds of larger social changes that are necessary to support the variety of family forms that are developing in the contemporary United States. By consciously affirming loving and supporting relations that go beyond the biological or legal family, by rejecting rigid domestic roles based on sex and age, collective families can offer models to many. Some communal strategies for survival can ease the lives of the millions of people living in single-parent households, step-families, or homes with two parents in the paid work force.

The numerous attempts that people have made to form intentional alternative families show how human beings can and do make conscious decisions about structuring their most intimate relationships. Most clearly, the search for alternatives illustrates that the family is a flexible institution. It is what human beings make of it. And every generation consciously or unconsciously contributes to shaping family form and ideology. Knowledge of the visionary schemes and living experiments of the past, together with the variety of life styles being lived in the present, gives us a fuller sense of the possibilities and choices before us and of our own power to shape our lives.

About the Authors

AMY SWERDLOW has directed two summer institutes on women's history for high school teachers, one at Sarah Lawrence College and the other at Stanford University. She was associate director of the women's studies program at Sarah Lawrence and was on the faculty of the Women's History Institute for Women's Organization Leaders. Swerdlow, who has directed many conferences, including two on women and the family, is the editor of *Feminist Perspectives on Housework and Child Care: A Conference Report.* She has four children and is currently working on her Ph.D. dissertation at Rutgers University.

RENATE BRIDENTHAL, who has a Ph.D. in history from Columbia University, is an associate professor of history at Brooklyn College of the City University of New York. Bridenthal was a founder and coordinator of the Brooklyn College women's studies program and a co-founder of the City University Women's Coalition. She has served as national co-chairwoman of the Coordinating Committee of Women in the Historical Profession and as convenor of the Conference Group in Women's History. Bridenthal is co-editor of *Becoming Visible: Women in European History* and is on the editorial Board of *Science and Society.*

JOAN KELLY is a professor of history at City College of New York. She is also on the doctoral faculty of the Graduate Center of the City University of New York and was a founding member of the Women in Society seminar at Columbia University. Kelly, who has a Ph.D. in history from Columbia University, has written and lectured extensively on Renaissance history, women's history, and feminist theory. She was a member of the national advisory board of the Sarah Lawrence Institute for the Integration of Women's History into the High School Curriculum.

PHYLLIS VINE teaches American history—including the history of the family—at Sarah Lawrence College. She received a Ph.D. in history from the University of Michigan and has written several articles on the history of higher education. Vine, who was assistant project director at the Institute for Social Research at the University of Michigan, co-authored two volumes for the Department of Health, Education and Welfare on desegregation and integration of secondary schools in the United States. She is currently completing a book on how families cope with mental illness.

Notes

Family Life:
A Historical Perspective

1. Claude Lévi-Strauss, "The Family," in H. Shapiro, ed., *Man, Culture, and Society* (London: Oxford University Press, 1971). His large study of tribal society is *The Elementary Structures of Kinship* (Boston: Beacon Press, 1969). For a critical evaluation, see Eleanor B. Leacock, "Structuralism and Dialectics," *Reviews in Anthropology* 5, 1 (Winter 1978): 117–28.

There are several useful studies of domestic arrangements in band and tribal societies in two anthropological collections: Rayna Rapp Reiter, ed., *Toward an Anthropology of Women* (New York: Monthly Review Press, 1975), and Michelle Rosaldo and Louise Lamphere, eds., *Woman, Culture, and Society* (Stanford, Calif.: Stanford University Press, 1974).

For the history of childhood, the classic study is Philippe Ariès, *Centuries of Childhood. A Social History of Family Life* (New York: Vintage Books, 1962). See also, Lloyd de Mause, ed., *The History of Childhood* (New York: Harper & Row, 1975), and John R. Gillis, *Youth and History* (New York: Academic Press, 1974).

For younger readers see Barbara Kaye Greenleaf, *Children Through the Ages: A History of Childhood* (New York: Barnes & Noble Books, 1979).

For lucid definitions and analysis of "family," "kin," and "household," see Rayna Rapp, "Family and Class Contemporary America," *Science and Society* XLII, 3 (Fall 1978): 278–300.

2. On the Lovedu, see Karen Sacks, "Engels Revisited," in Reiter, ed., *Toward an Anthropology of Women*, p. 225. On the Fou, see Melville Herskovits, *Dahomey* (Evanston, Ill.: Northwestern University Press, 1967), pp. 320–22. For other instances of female husbands and male wives, see Denise O'Brien, "Female Husbands in Southern Bantu Societies," in Alice Schlegel, ed., *Sexual Stratification. A Cross-Cultural View* (New York: Columbia University Press, 1977), and Gayle Rubin, "The Traffic in Women," in Reiter, ed., *Toward an Anthropology of Women*, p. 181.

3. Eleanor Leacock, "Women in Egalitarian Societies," in Renate Bridenthal and Claudia Koonz, eds., *Becoming Visible: Women in European History* (Boston: Houghton Mifflin, 1977), pp. 11–35.

4. Nancy Tanner, "Matrifocality in Indonesia and Africa and Among Black Americans," in Rosaldo and Lamphere, eds., *Woman, Culture, and Society*, pp. 129–56.

5. The classic study of European feudal society is Marc Bloch, *Feudal Society* (Chicago: University of Chicago Press, 1964), 2 vols. Also useful are Sidney Painter, *French Chivalry* (Baltimore: Johns Hopkins Press, 1940), and Eileen Power, *Medieval Women* (Cambridge: Cambridge University Press, 1975).

6. For medieval romances, see *Arthurian Romances*, trans. and ed. by W.W. Comfort (London and New York: Dutton and Dutton Everyman's Library, 1970) and *Lays of Marie de France* (London and New York: Dent and Dutton, 1911). Poems by women troubadours are in *The Women Troubadours*, trans. and ed. by Meg Bogin (New York: Paddington Press, 1976).

On courtly love, see Joan Kelly-Gadol, "Did Women Have a Renaissance?" in Bridenthal and Koonz, eds., *Becoming Visible*, pp. 137–64; Emily James Putnam, *The Lady* (Chicago: University of Chicago Press, 1970), chap. 4; and Maurice Valency, *In Praise of Love* (New York: Macmillan, 1961).

7. On the Church and universities, good introductions are Marshall W. Baldwin, *The Mediaeval Church* (Ithaca, N.Y.: Cornell University Press, 1953); Geoffrey Barraclough, *The Medieval Papacy* (New York: Harcourt Brace, 1968); and Helen Waddell, *The Wandering Scholars* (London: Constable, 1932).

8. On serfdom, see G.G. Coulton, *Medieval Village, Manor, and Monastery* (New York: Harper & Row, 1960). Medieval history and its institutional development are best presented by Henri Pirenne, *A History of Europe* (New York: Anchor Books, 1958), 2 vols.

9. A basic, very readable work on the preindustrial family is Louise Tilly and Joan Scott, *Women, Work, and Family* (New York: Holt, Rinehart & Winston, 1978. For reference, see Lawrence Stone, *The Family, Sex and Marriage in England, 1500-1800* (New York: Harper & Row, 1977.

10. Stone, *The Family, Sex and Marriage*, p. 156.

11. Doris Mary Stenton, *The English Woman in History* (New York: Schocken Books, 1977), p. 117; Stone, *The Family, Sex and Marriage*, p. 199.

12. For a good collection of articles on the family in Europe and the United States, see Michael Gordon, ed., *The American Family in Perspective* (New York: St. Martin's Press, 1973). See especially the essays by John Demos and Edmund Morgan on New England.

13. On the black family, see Andrew Billingsley and Amy Tate Billingsley, *Black Families in White*

America (Englewood Cliffs, N.J.: Prentice-Hall, 1968); John W. Blassingame, *The Slave Community* (New York: Oxford University Press, 1972); Herbert G. Gutman, *The Black Family in Slavery and Freedom, 1750-1925* (New York: Random House, 1977); and Carol B. Stack, *All Our Kin* (New York: Harper & Row, 1974).

14. Gutman, *The Black Family*, p. 6.

15. Jim Watts and Allen F. Davis, *Generations: Your Family in Modern American History* (New York: Alfred A. Knopf, 1978), p. 201.

16. On bourgeois women and the women's movement, see Barbara Corrado Pope, "Angels in the Devil's Workshop: Leisured and Charitable Women in Nineteenth Century England and France," in Bridenthal and Koonz, eds., *Becoming Visible*, pp. 296–324, and Edith Hurwitz, "The International Sisterhood," in *Becoming Visible*, pp. 325–45.

17. On the bourgeois family, see Eli Zaretsky, *Capitalism, the Family, and Personal Life* (New York: Harper & Row, 1976).

18. On nineteenth- and twentieth-century working children and wives, see the later chapters of Tilly and Scott, *Women, Work, and Family*; also Mary Lynn McDougall, "Working-Class Women During the Industrial Revolution, 1780-1914," in Bridenthal and Koonz, eds., *Becoming Visible*, pp. 255–79, and Theresa M. McBride, "The Long Road Home: Women's Work and Industrialization," in *Becoming Visible*, pp. 255–80.

For the United States, see Rosalyn Baxandall, Linda Gordon, and Susan Reverby, eds., *America's Working Women* (New York: Random House, 1976), and Mary Ryan, *Womanhood in America from Colonial Times to the Present* (New York: Franklin Watts, 1975).

19. Ryan, *Womanhood in America*, p. 207.

20. Ann Oakley, *The Sociology of Housework* (New York: Random House, 1974), pp. 92–95.

21. Tilly and Scott, *Women, Work, and Family*, pp. 46, 58.

22. Margaret Mead, *Sex and Temperament in Three Primitive Societies* (New York: Dell, 1971), p.55.

23. Oakley, *Sociology of Housework*, p. 93.

24. 1979 figures for the typical 99.6-hour week of a housewife/mother, if paid at the minimum wage for each each of her tasks, comes to $351.66 a week or $18,286.32 a year. New York *Daily News*, 25 February 1979.

25. Oakley, *Sociology of Housework*, pp. 136–41.

26. *Comment* 11, 1 (September 1978): 1, and Z.I. Giraldo and J.M. Weatherford, *Life Cycle and the American Family: Current Trends and Policy Implications* (Durham, N.C.: Duke University Institute of Policy Sciences and Public Affairs, Policy Paper #1 of the Center for the Study of Family and the State, 1978), p. 3-1.

27. U.S. Bureau of the Census, *A Statistical Portrait of Women in the U.S.* (Washington, D.C.: Department of Commerce, Bureau of the Census, 1977), Current Population Reports, Special Studies Series P-23, NO. 58, pp. 28, 30, 31.

28. Ibid., p. 45.

29. Department of Labor projections are that women will constitute 51.4 percent of the labor force by 1990. See Giraldo and Weatherford, *Life Cycle*, p. 3-10.

30. Ibid., pp. 3-7, 3-8.

31. Gutman, *The Black Family*, p. 530.

32. Giraldo and Weatherford, *Life Cycle*, pp. 1-1-1-15.

33. Stenton, *The English Woman*, p. 153. For the family patterns of preindustrial Europe, see Tilly and Scott, *Women, Work, and Family*, and Stone, *The Family, Sex, and Marriage.*

34. Tilly and Scott, *Women, Work, and Family*, p. 28.

35. Giraldo and Weatherford, *Life Cycle*, pp. 1-16, 1-8; Mary Jo Bane, *Here to Stay: The American Family in the Twentieth Century* (New York: Basic Books, 1976), p. 76.

36. Ad Hoc Women's Studies Committee Against Sterilization Abuse, *Workbook on Sterilization and Sterilization Abuse* (Bronxville, N.Y.: Sarah Lawrence Publications, 1978); Committee for Abortion Rights and Against Sterilization Abuse, *Women Under Attack: Abortion, Sterilization Abuse, and Reproductive Freedom* (New York: CARASA, P.O. Box 124, Cathedral Station).

37. *Options*, the Newsletter of the Religious Coalition for Abortion Rights, published in Washington, D.C. (100 Maryland Ave., NE), regularly carries information of this kind.

The Family Tree: Contemporary Patterns

1. Z.I. Giraldo and J.M. Weatherford, *Life Cycle and the American Family: Current Trends and Policy Implications* (Durham, N.C.: Duke University Institute of Policy Science and Public Affairs, Policy Paper #1 of the Center for the Study of Family and the State, 1978), p. 1-1

2. Mary Jo Bane, *Here to Stay: American Families in the Twentieth Century* (New York: Basic Books, 1976).

3. "New Directions," *Journal of Home Economics*, May 1975, p. 6.

4. Rayna Rapp, Ellen Ross, and Renate Bridenthal, "Examining Family History," *Feminist Studies*, 5,1 (Spring 1979). Also Rayna Rapp, "Family and Class in Contemporary

America: Notes Toward an
Understanding of Ideology," *Science
and Society*, XLII, 3 (Fall 1978).

5. W. Lloyd Warner and Paul S.
Lunt, *The Social Life of a Modern
Community* (New Haven, Conn.:
Yale University Press, 1941), p. 72.

6. Ferdinand Lundberg, *The Rich
and the Super-Rich* (New York:
Bantam Books, 1968), p. 210.

7. Percentages are from U.S.
Bureau of the Cenus, *Statistical
Abstract of the United States: 1978*
(Washington, D.C.:Department of
Commerce, Bureau of the Census,
1978) p.453. The shape of the chart,
and information on the above-
$25,000 earners, is adapted from a
larger, more detailed chart by
Stephen Rose and Dennis
Livingston, "Social Stratification in
the U.S." (Baltimore: Social Graphics
Co., 1978)

8. *San Francisco Sunday Examiner
and Chronicle*, citing U.S. Census
figures, 30 July 1978; Kenneth
Keniston and The Carnegie Council
on Children, *All Our Children*
(New York: Harcourt Brace
Jovanovich, 1977).

9. Peter Collier and David
Horowitz, *The Rockefellers, An
American Dynasty* (New York: Holt,
Rinehart & Winston, 1976), p. 592.

10. Rosalind Petchesky, "Workers,
Reproductive Hazards, and the
Politics of Protection: An
Introduction," *Feminist Studies* 5, 2
(Summer 1979): 244.

11. *Economic Notes*, April–May
1979 (publication of the Labor
Research Association), p. 2.

12. Bureau of the Census,
Statistical Abstract: 1978,
p. 446.

13. Richard H. de Lone, *Small
Futures: Children, Inequality, and
the Limits of Liberal Reform* (New
York: Harcourt Brace Jovanovich,
1979), p. 3.

14. Bureau of the Census,
Statistical Abstract: 1978, p. 453.

15. Ibid., pp. 452, 453, 456.

16. Ibid., p. 494.

17. Figures are taken from the
Bureau of the Census, *Statistical
Abstract: 1978*, p. 494. The format of
the interpretation is based on charts
in Kenneth Keniston and The
Carnegie Council, *All Our Children*,
pp. 29–30.

18. David E. Koskoff, *The
Mellons, The Chronicle of America's
Richest Family* (New York: Thomas
Y. Crowell, 1978), p. 475.

19. *Wall Street Journal*, 23 August
1979.

20. Mary Jo Bane, *Here to Stay*,
p. 16.

21. Giraldo and Weatherford, *Life
Cycle*, p. 1–5.

22. Collier and Horowitz, *The
Rockefellers*, p. 509.

23. Nathaniel Burt, *First Families:
The Making of an American
Aristocracy* (Boston and Toronto:
Little, Brown, 1970), p. 414.

24. Stephen Birmingham, *The
Right People* (Boston: Little, Brown,
1968).

25. Robert Coles, *Privileged Ones:
The Well-off and the Rich in
America*, vol. 5 of *Children of Crisis*
(Boston: Little, Brown, 1977), p. 71.

26. Ibid., p. 534.

27. Ibid., p. 536.

28. Ludwig Geismar, *555
Families: A Social-Psychological
Study of Young Families in
Transition* (New Brunswick, N.J.:
Transaction Books, 1973), p. 92.

29. Carol B. Stack, *All Our Kin:
Strategies for Survival in a Black
Community* (New York: Harper &
Row, 1974).

30. *New York Times*, 9
September 1979.

31. Paul Wilkes, *Trying Out the
Dream* (New York: Warner Books,
1976).

32. Frances E. Kobrin and Calvin
Goldscheider, *The Ethnic Factor in
Family Structure and Mobility*
(Cambridge, Mass.: Ballinger, 1978).

33. Koskoff, *The Mellons*, p. 527.

34. Susan Sheehan, *A Welfare Mother* (New York: The New American Library, 1975, 1976), pp. 89–99.

35. Vance Packard, *The Status Seekers* (New York: Pocket Books, 1959), p. 129.

36. Skolnick and Skolnick, "Battered Wives," in *Violence in the Family*, Suzanne K. Steinmetz and Murray A. Strauss, eds. (New York: Harper & Row, 1974).

37. Lillian Breslow Rubin, *Worlds of Pain: Life in the Working-Class Family* (New York: Basic Books, 1976), p. 29.

38. Ibid., pp. 207–9.

39. Elliot Liebow, *Tally's Corner* (Boston: Little, Brown, 1967), chaps. 3, 4. E.E. LeMasters, *Blue-Collar Aristocrats* (Madison, Wis.: University of Wisconsin Press, 1975).

40. Richard Sennett and Jonathan Cobb, *The Hidden Injuries of Class* (New York: Alfred A. Knopf/Vintage Books, 1972).

41. Liebow, *Tally's Corner*, chap. 3; Stack, *All Our Kin*.

42. Stack, *All Our Kin*, chap. 6.

43. Agnes Smedley, *Daughter of Earth* (1929; reprint ed., Old Westbury, N.Y.: Feminist Press, 1973).

44. Coles, *Privileged Ones*, p. 390.

45. Ibid., pp. 63, 107, 273, pt. V, no. 6.

46. Sophy Burnham, *The Landed Gentry* (New York: G.P. Putnam's Sons, 1978), p. 260.

47. Ibid., p. 266.

48. Coles, *Privileged Ones*, pp. 83–89.

49. Ibid., p. 352.

50. Burnham, *Landed Gentry*, p. 20.

51. Burton Hersh, *The Mellon Family* (New York: William Morrow, 1978), p. 426.

52. Louis Auchincloss, *A Writer's Capital* (Minneapolis, Minn.: University of Minnesota Press, 1974), pp. 45–46.

53. Coles, *Privileged Ones*.

54. Auchincloss, *Writer's Capital*; Coles, *Privileged Ones*, pt. V, no. 1.

55. Coles, *Privileged Ones*, pt. VI.

56. Stephen Birmingham, *Certain People: America's Black Elite* (Boston: Little, Brown, 1977), p. 58.

57. Coles, *Privileged Ones*, p. 354.

58. National Urban League, *Black Families in the 1974–75 Depression* (Washington, D.C.: National Urban League Research Department, 1975).

59. Ibid.

60. Bureau of the Census, *Statistical Abstract: 1978*, p. 453.

61. Ibid., p. 446.

62. National Urban League, *Black Families*; Gerald R. Leslie, *The Family in Social Context* (New York: Oxford University Press, 1975).

63. Leo Grebler, Joan W. Moore, and Ralph G. Guzman, eds., *The Mexican-American People* (New York: Free Press, 1963, 1970), chap. 15.

64. Ibid.

65. Marc Feigen Fasteau, *The Male Machine* (New York: Dell, 1975), p. 36.

66. Sennett and Cobb, *The Hidden Injuries*, p. 114.

67. Ibid., p. 50.

68. Rubin, *Worlds of Pain*, p. 97.

69. U.S. Bureau of the Census. *Statistical Abstract of the United States: 1977* (Washington, D.C.: Department of Commerce, Bureau of the Census, 1977), pp. 38–40.

70. *New York Times*, 27 June 1979, citing study from the U.S. Bureau of the Census.

71. Ibid.

72. Ruth Cavan, *The American Family*, 3d. ed. (New York: Thomas Y. Crowell, 1963), p. 204.

73. Bureau of the Census, *Statistical Abstract: 1977*, p. 50; Kobrin and Goldscheider, *The Ethnic Factor*, chap. 6.

74. Bert N. Adams, *The American Family* (Chicago: Markham Publishing Co., 1971), p. 209.

75. Kobrin and Goldscheider, *The Ethnic Factor*, chap. 6.

76. *Personal letter to the author.*

77. *New York Times*, 30 January 1978, quoting Roger Lazey and Richard C. Levy, *Wife Beating.*

78. Thomas J. Cottle, *A Family Album, Portraits of Intimacy and Kinship* (New York: Harper & Row, 1974), pp. 138–39.

79. *New York Times*, 8 July 1979.

80. *San Francisco Chronicle*, 2 July 1979.

81. Heather L. Ross and Isabel V. Sawhill, *Time of Transition, The Growth of Families Headed by Women* (Washington, D.C.: Urban Institute, 1975), pp. 173–80.

82. Robert O. Blood, Jr., and Donald M. Wolfe, *Husbands and Wives: The Dynamics of Married Living* (New York: Free Press, 1960).

83. Rubin, *Worlds of Pain*, pp. 222, 224, 225.

84. Giraldo and Weatherford, *Life Cycle.*

85. *New York Times*, 27 June 1979, citing study from the U.S. Bureau of the Census.

86. Ibid.

87. Lucia H. Bequaert, *Single Women, Alone and Together* (Boston: Beacon Press, 1976), p. 3.

88. Ibid., p. 95.

89. Ibid., p. 80.

90. Ibid.

91. *New York Times*, 26 June 1979.

92. Ginny Vida, *Our Right to Love: A Lesbian Resource Book* (Englewood Cliffs, N.J.: Prentice-Hall, 1978), pp. 56–77.

93. Boston Women's Health Book Collective, *Ourselves and Our Children* (New York: Random House, 1978), p. 175.

94. Bureau of the Census, *Statistical Abstract: 1977*, p. 41; *New York Times*, 27 November 1977.

95. Arthur Sorosky, Annette Baran, and Reuben Pannor, *The Adoption Triangle* (New York: Doubleday/Anchor, 1978).

96. Donnell M. Pappenfort, Dee Morgan Kilpatrick, and Robert W. Roberts, eds., *Child Caring* (Chicago: Aldine Publishing, 1973).

97. Wilkes, *Trying Out the Dream*, p. 298.

98. Pappenfort, Kilpatrick, and Roberts, *Child Caring.*

99. *New York Times*, 30 July 1978, p. F16.

100. Bureau of the Census, *Statistical Abstract: 1977*, p. 29.

101. *New York Times*, 7 May 1978.

102. Giraldo and Weatherford, *Life Cycle*, p. 5-3.

103. Bane, *Here To Stay*, p. 40.

104. Vida, *Our Right to Love*, p. 234.

105. Cavan, *The American Family*, p. 508.

The Search for Alternatives: Past, Present, and Future

1. For an interpretative description of alternative societies by utopian writers, painters, poets, and architects, see Ian Tod and Michael Wheeler, *Utopia* (New York: Harmony Books, 1978), and Rosabeth Moss Kanter, *Commitment and Community: Communes and Utopias in Sociological Perspective* (Cambridge, Mass.: Harvard University Press, 1972).

2. Thomas More, *Utopia*, trans. and ed. by Robert Adams (1516; reprint ed., New York: W.W. Norton, 1975), pp. 65–66.

3. Tomasso Campanella, *The City of the Sun*, in Robert L. Chienese, ed., *Peaceable Kingdoms: An Anthology of Utopian Writing* (New York: Harcourt Brace Jovanovich, 1971), pp. 7–43.

4. J.F.C. Harrison, *Quest for the New Moral World* (New York:

Charles Scribner's Sons, 1969), p. 59, quoted from *New Harmony Gazette*, October 1825. Other useful introductions to utopian thought or communitarian experiments include: Arthur Bestor, *Backwoods Utopia: The Sectarian and Owenite Phase of Communitarian Socialism in America, 1663-1829* (Philadelphia: University of Pennsylvania Press, 1970); Mark Holloway, *Heavens on Earth: Utopian Communities in America, 1680-1880* (London: Turnstile Press, 1951); Dolores Hayden, *Seven American Utopias: The Architecture of Communitarian Socialism, 1790-1925* (Cambridge, Mass.: M.I.T. Press, 1976); Charles Nordhoff, *The Communistic Societies of the United States* (New York: Schocken Books, 1975); and Robert S. Fogerty, *American Utopianism* (Itasca, Ill.: F.E. Peacock Publishers, 1972).

5. A.J.G. Perkins and Theresa Wolfson, *Frances Wright: Free Enquirer* (Philadelphia: Porcupine Press, 1972), p. 150.

6. Ibid., pp. 193-94.

7. William M. Kephart, "Experimental Family Organization: An Historico-Cultural Report on the Oneida Community," in Michael Gordon, ed., *The Nuclear Family in Crisis: The Search for an Alternative* (New York: Harper & Row, 1972), p. 62.

8. For an excellent discussion of sex·roles and women in Oneida, see Louis J. Kern, "Ideology and Reality: Sexuality and Women's Status in the Oneida Community," *Radical History Review*, 20 (Spring/Summer 1979):181-206. For firsthand accounts of Oneida, see Constance Noyes Robertson, *The Oneida Community: An Autobiography, 1851-1876* (Syracuse, N.Y.: Syracuse University Press, 1970), and Pierpont B. Noyes, *My Father's House: An Oneida Boyhood* (New York: Farrar and Rinehart, 1937).

9. Dolores Hayden, "Two Utopian Feminists and Their Campaigns for Kitchenless Houses," *Signs*, 4,2 (Winter 1978):274-90.

10. Charlotte Perkins Gilman, *The Home: Its Work and Influence* (1903; reprint ed., Chicago: University of Chicago Press, 1972), pp. 132-33.

11. Charlotte Perkins Gilman, *Herland* (1915; reprint ed., with an intro. by Ann J. Lane, New York: Pantheon Books, 1979).

12. Frederick Engels, *The Origin of the Family, Private Property and the State* (1884; reprint ed., New York: International Publishers, 1973), p. 120.

13. Ibid., p. 129.

14. Ibid. See also August Bebel, *Woman Under Socialism* (1883; reprint ed., New York: Schocken Books, 1971).

15. Yonina Talmon, "Family Life in the Kibbutz: From Revolutionary Days to Stabilization," in Rosabeth Moss Kanter, ed., *Communes: Creating and Managing the Collective Life* (New York: Harper & Row, 1973), pp. 327-28.

16. A.I. Rabin, "Kibbutz Child-Rearing and Personality Development," in Kanter, ed., *Communes*, p. 390.

17. Yonina Talmon, "Aging in Israel, A Planned Society," in Gordon, ed., *The Nuclear Family in Crisis*, p. 106.

18. Louise Lamphere, *Anthropology Resource Center*, June 1979, p.1.

19. *New York Times*, 29 November 1976, p. 28.

20. Margaret Randall, *Cuban Women Now: An Afterword, 1974* (Toronto: The Women's Press, 1974), p. 11.

21. Statement by Vilma Espin at

Press Conference in Havana, Cuba, March 1975, as reported by Margaret Randall in "Objective and Subjective Factors in Women's Oppression: 1974 Campaign Against Sexism in Cuba" (Havana, 1978, unpublished paper).

22. Karen Wald, *Children of Che* (Palo Alto, Calif.: Ramparts Press, 1978), pp. 126, 132.

23. Bror Rexed, "The Children's World and Ours," *Current Sweden*, May 1976, pp. 3, 4.

24. Camilla Odhnoff, "Equality Is for Children, Too," *Current Sweden*, March 1976, p. 2.

25. Rita Liljestrom, Gunilla Furst Mellstrom, and Gillan Liljestrom Svenson, *Sex Roles in Transition* (Stockholm: Swedish Institute, 1975), p. 15.

26. Elisabet Sandberg, *Equality is the Goal* (Stockholm: The Swedish Institute, 1973), p. 44.

27. Lillemor Melsted, *Swedish Family Policy* (New York: Swedish Information Service, 1979), p. 5.

28. Sheila B. Kamerman, "Work and Family in Industrialized Societies," *Signs*, 4,4 (Summer 1979):649.

29. Sandberg, *Equality Is the Goal*, p. 71.

30. Melsted, *Swedish Family Policy*, p. 4.

31. Brigitta Wittorp and Karen Lund, "Some Facts about Swedish Children and Their Parents," *Current Sweden*, May 1976, p. 4.

32. Ulla Jacobson, *A Child's Rights* (Stockholm: Askeld & Karnehull, 1978).

33. Ulla Jacobson, "The Child Parent Relationship," *Current Sweden*, 224 (June 1979):10.

34. Liljestrom et. al., *Sex Roles in Transition*, pp. 52–72.

35. Sandberg, *Equality Is the Goal*, p. 83.

36. James A. Levine, *Who Will Raise the Children: New Options for*

Fathers (Philadelphia: J.B. Lippincott, 1976).

37. *New York Times*, 8 January 1980, p. B5.

38. UPI, *City News*, 23 October 1978.

39. Levine, *Who Will Raise the Children*, pp. 83–87.

40. *Women: A Journal of Liberation*, 4,3 (undated):40.

41. Benjamin Spock, *Baby and Child Care* (New York: Pocket Books, 1976 ed.), p. xix.

42. Quoted in Levine, *Who Will Raise the Children*, p. 192.

43. Selma G. Lanes, "Communes: A Firsthand Report on a Controversial New Life Style," *Parents Magazine*, October 1971, p. 63.

44. *New York Times*, 8 September 1977, p. B7.

45. Neta Jackson, "Our Commune in Suburbia," *Redbook*, January 1972, p. 44.

46. M. Young and J. Young, "Can Group Family Life Work?" *Parents Magazine*, August 1973, pp. 42–43.

47. Bennet M. Berger, et. al., "Child-Rearing Practices of the Communal Family," in Arlene S. Skolnick and Jerome H. Skolnick, eds., *Family in Transition* (Boston: Little, Brown, 1970), pp. 476–501, and Bennet M. Berger, et. al., "Supporting the Communal Family," in Kanter, ed., *Communes*, p. 248.

48. Elizabeth Bernhart, "Friends and Lovers in a Lesbian Counterculture Community," in Nona Glazer-Malbin, ed., *Old Family/New Family: Interpersonal Relationships* (New York: D. Van Nostrand, 1975), pp. 90–115.

49. Ginny Vida, *Our Right to Love: A Lesbian Resource Book* (Englewood Cliffs, N.J.: Prentice-Hall, 1978), p. 68.

50. Rosabeth Moss Kanter, "Communes in Cities," in John Case and Rosemary C.R. Taylor, eds., *Co-*

ops, Communes, and Collectives
(New York: Pantheon Books, 1979),
p. 122.

51. Bennet Berger, "The Decline
of Age Grading in Rural Anarchist
Communes," paper presented at the
American Sociological Association,
New Orleans, August 1972, quoted
in Jessie Bernard, *The Future of
Motherhood* (New York: Penguin
Books, 1974), p. 316.

52. Bernard, *The Future of
Motherhood*, p. 317.

53. Michael Weiss, *Living
Together* (New York: McGraw-Hill,
1974), p. 133.

54. Sandra Boston, Allan Tuttle,
and Firefly, "Are We a Family? Living
and Loving with Kids at Rainbow
Community," *Communities*, 27
(July/August 1977): 4–5.

55. Ibid.,p. 16.

Index

The numbers in italics indicate pages with photographs.

abortion, 40, 41; *see also* birth control
adoption (of children), 99–100
adultery, 6
aged and aging: family and, 42–43, 101–105; kibbutz movement and, 127, 130; *see also* retirement
Agins, Judy, 147–148
Aid to Families with Dependent Children, 100; *see also* social services; welfare
Alcoa Company, 55
alcohol, 80
alienation, 108
All Our Children (Keniston), 58
ancestry, 55; *see also* kinship
Arapesh people, 29
arranged marriages, 91; *see also* family; marriage
Atjehnese people, 4, 10
Austria, 101

Baby and Child Care (Spock), 75, 145–146
Bellamy, Edward, 122
Berger, Bennet, 152, 154
Bernard, Jessie, 154
birth, 142
birth control, 40–41, 42, 44–45; celibacy, 7, 117–118; Noyes, 119; Owen, 114; poverty, 64
birth rate declines, 39, 40–41, 62–63
blacks: family income, 57; family size, 63; family structure, 85–86; Nashoba, 115–116; slavery, 11, 14, 25; upper class, 82, 84; *see also* race
bloomer costume, 114
bourgeois family, 18–22, 24; child care in, 29; *see also* upper class; upper middle class
bourgeoisie, 10
Bridenthal, Renate, xvii, xx, 47–105

California, 98
Campanella, Tomasso, 108, 112
capital: division of labor, 18–19; family control, 53; nuclear family, 16, 32; social class, 50–51
capitalism, 124
Catholics: family size, 63; marriage, 91; *see also* religion
Celanese Corporation, 83
celibacy, 7; Shakers, 117–118; *see also* birth control
Chase Manhattan Bank, 55
Chicanos, 76, 85, 86–87
child abuse, 93
childbirth, 142
child care and rearing, 94, *129*; bourgeois, 20; communal, 100, 101, 110, 114, 119–120, 153–156; Cuba, 134–135; family size and, 39; feudalism, 5; housework and, 27–30 (*see also* housework); kibbutz movement, 127; Marxism, 124–125; poverty, 66; preindustrial, 11; sex role and, 29, 133–140, 142–146; tribal societies, 3–4; U.S., 141–146; wage-earning mothers, 35, 63; *see also* day-care centers
child labor, 80, 117, 140
child labor laws, 23
children: adoption, 99–100; bourgeois family, 21; divorce rights of, 140; homosexual custody rights, 98, 99; institutionalized, 100–101; marriage and, 95; opportunities of, 58, 62; servants and, 66, 71; sexuality of, 117; socialization of, 69–84 (*see also* socialization); working class, 22–23 (*see also* working class)
Child's Right to Divorce, A (Jacobson), 141
Church, *see* religion

City of the Sun, The (Campanella), 108, 112

class, *see* social class

cohabitation: increase in, 90, 96–97; law and, 98

coitus interruptus, 119; *see also* birth control

communes and communitarian societies, 107, 157, 158, 159; aging, 104–105; child care, 100, 101, 110; contemporary, 146–157; counterculture, 151–157; kibbutz movement, 125–131; *see also* utopias

Communities (journal), 156

Community (Portland, Oregon), 152–153

companionate marriage, 92, 96; *see also* family; marriage.

conspicuous consumption, 19

consumerism, 108

contraception, *see* birth control

corporations, 108

counterculture communes, 151–157

courtly love, 6–7

craft production, 10

Cuba, 101, 133–136, 157

dating, 91

day-care centers, 35–36, 95, *129*; Cuba, 135; Sweden, 139

death rate, *see* mortality rates

debt, 58

Defoe, Daniel, 11

dependency: bourgeois family, 20–21; marriage and, 126; nuclear family, 33; sex role, 36

Depression of 1929–1939, 56

desertion, 78

discrimination: homosexuals, 99; social mobility and, 84, 85; women, 139

division of labor: child care, 29; communes, 149; industrialization, 17; nuclear family, 18–26, 27–33; sex role, 36–38, 132–133, 141, 157; working-class family, 23, 26

divorce, 44; bourgeois family, 20; child from parents, 140; Cuba,

135–136; family stability, 37; marriage and, 93–94; mortality rates, 39, 40, 48; poverty, 57; single-parent families, 64; working class, 95–96

Doll's House, A (Ibsen), 22

Douglass, Frederick, 84

dowry, 39

drug abuse, 80

Du Pont family, 55, 65–66

eating habits, 73

education: compulsory, 23; family roles, 29–30; feudal society, 6, 8; nuclear family, 33, 44; social mobility, 67; upper class, 82–83

Engels, Frederick, 124–125, 126

England, 39

Enlightenment, 112

entitlement, 83

Eskimo people, 40

Espin, Vilma, 134

eugenic breeding, 110, 112, 119

extended family, xvi, xvii, xx, 48, 66–67; Cuba, 135; decline of, 17–18, 38, 62, 65; geographic mobility, 67; poverty, 79; *see also* family; household

Exxon Corporation, 51

factory system: nuclear household, 15, 16, 17; utopias, 113

family: aging, 42–43, 101–105; anthropological definition, 1; blacks, 85–86 (*see also* blacks); bourgeois, 18–22, 29; budgets, 59–61; Chicanos, 86–87; childless, 42; consumption role, xviii, 2, 19, 26; definitions of, xvi–xviii, 1, 47–50; extended, 38, 48, 62, 65, 67, 79, 135; Fourier, 116; household composition, 62–68; household distinguished from, 48; housework, 26–32 (*see also* housework); Marxism, 124–125; More, 111–112; nuclear (*see* nuclear family); Owen, 114; Plato, 110–112; reorganizational schemes, 121–122; slavery, 14;

social class and, 50–62 (*see also* social class); socialization in, 68–90 (*see also* socialization); social welfare role, xviii; types of, 2–15; violence in, 74, 93; Wright, 115; *see also* household

family size, 38–39, 41, 44, 63, 87; decrease in, 48, 62; norms, 68

Family, The (Lévi-Strauss), 1

feminism, xx, 114, 157; communitarians, 108–109, 156; kibbutz movement, 126; *see also* sex role; women's movement

fertility rates, *see* birth rates

feudal society, xix, 4–9, 18

First National City Bank, 83

"flex-time," 143, 158

food stamps, 57, 102

Ford family, 55

Ford Motor Company, 55

Fou people, 3

Fourier, Charles, 113, 116–117, 124

Freud, Sigmund, 22, 117

France, 39

French Revolution, 13

Frost, Robert, xviii

gay movement, *see* homosexuality; lesbianism

gender identification, *see* men; sex role; women

General Motors Corporation, 55

geographic mobility, 67; *see also* social mobility

Gilman, Charlotte Perkins, 121–123, 157

Ginzberg, Eli, 131

Greece, 4

Groton School, 83

Gulf Oil Corporation, 55

Hacket, Bruce M., 152

Haiti, 116

Harvard University, 83

Herland (Gilman), 122–123

Hispanics: discrimination, 85; family size, 63

Home, The (Gilman), 122

homogamy, 91–92

homosexuality, 1, 42, 98–99, 116; aging, 103; child care, 144–145; communes, 152–153; Cuba, 136; marriage, 91

household: composition of, 62–68; family definition and, xvi, 48; heads of, xvii–xviii; industrialization and, 17; nuclear family development, 15; preindustrial, 9–15; single-parent, xvii–xviii, xix; *see also* family

housework, 26–32, 94, 157; Marxism, 124–125; Noyes, 120; retirement, 103; wages for, 30–32, 121–122

IBM, 51

Ibsen, Henrik, 22

income distribution, 52–62; aging, 101–102, 104; median income, 57; race, 86; *see also* social class

indentured servants, 11, 14

industrialization: family, 15–16, 17–18; utopias, 113

industrial revolution, 50, 51

infanticide, 15, 40

infant mortality, 39, 40, 64

inflation: living standards, 58; pensions; 102

inheritance, 140; bourgeois family, 20, 21; preindustrial society, 9, 10; upper class, 55

institutionalized children, 100–101

Iroquois people, 4, 10

Israel, 101; *see also* kibbutz movement

Jacobson, Ulla, 140

Japan, 5

Jews: family size, 63; kibbutz movement, 125–131; Orthodox, 91; *see also* religion

job sharing, 143, 158

Johnson, George, 84

Johnson, John, 84

Johnson Publishing Company, 84

Journal of Home Economics, xvii, 48, 49

Judaic-Christian tradition, xvii

Kamerman, Sheila, 139
Kelly, Joan, xx, xxi, 1–45
Keniston, Kenneth, 58
Kern, Louis J., 121
kibbutz movement, 125–131,
    132, 158
kinship, xvi, 2–4, 14

labor force: children in, 80, 117, 140;
    women in, xviii, 34–38, 44, 63, 94,
    109, 131–132
Lakey, Berit, 150
Lakey, George, 150, 151
land, see property
law: cohabitation, 98; homosexuality,
    98–99
Lee, Ann (Mother Lee), 118
Lee, Robert E., 84
Lesbian Community Center
    (Baltimore), 144–145
lesbianism, 42, 98–99, 128; aging,
    103; child care, 144–145;
    communes, 152–153; marriage, 91
Levine, James A., 142
Lévi-Strauss, Claude, 1
Liljestrom, Rita, 141
lineage, 13
living standards, 57–61
Looking Backward (Bellamy), 122
Louis, Joe, 84
Lovedu people, 3
lower middle class, 56; see also
    working class

machismo, 87, 134
male continence, 119; see also birth
    control
marriage: alternatives to, 96–99;
    companionate, 92, 96; conflicts
    in, 93–96; dependence in, 126;
    divorce and, 93–94 (see also
    divorce); extent of, 90; feudal
    society, 5, 6, 7; interracial, 91;
    kibbutz movement, 126; laws of,
    94; mate selection, 91–96;
    mobility and, 55, 73; preindustrial
    society, 12–13, 14; upper class,
    82–83

marriage age: changes in, 90; divorce
    and, 95–96; increase in, 97;
    preindustrial family, 39
Marvin, Lee, 98
Marx, Karl, 123–125
mate selection, 91–96
matriarchy, 85–86
matrilineality, 4, 10
Mead, Margaret, 29
median income, 57
medieval Europe, see feudal society
Medicare and Medicaid, 102
Mellon Bank, 55, 83
Mellon family, 55
men: bourgeois family, 20–21; child
    care role, 29–30, 35, 37, 44,
    133–136; power of, 51, 94; see
    also paternalism; patriarchy;
    sex role
middle class: aging, 102; child social-
    ization, 72–75; communitarians,
    108, 146–147; defined, 55–56;
    family budgets, 60, 61; marriage,
    92; sex role, 89; social mobil-
    ity, 67; see also bourgeois
    family; social class; entries
    under other classes
migrant farm workers, 79, 87
Mill, Harriet Taylor, 28
Miller, R. Mervyn, 152
mobility, see geographic mobility;
    social mobility
monogamy, 7, 108, 157; Campanella,
    112; communes, 148; Marxism,
    125; More, 111; Noyes, 118; Plato,
    110; serial, 152
monopolies, 108
More, Sir Thomas, 111
Mormons, 117, 118
mortality rates: declines in,
    39–40; divorce and, 39, 40, 48;
    poverty, 64
motherhood: teenagers, 64; tribal
    society, 3–4; see also child care
    and rearing
Movement for a New Society, 155

Nashoba community (Tenn.),
    115–116, 158

National Commission on Manpower
    Policy, 131
National Council for Alternative
    Work Patterns, 143
Native Americans, 63, 84
Nayar people, 1, 2
Nepal, 15
New England, 11–12
New Harmony (Ind.), 113–115
New Jersey Supreme Court, 98
New York City, 38
New York Times, 143, 147
Nightingale, Florence, 20
norms: family size, 63, 64, 68;
    nuclear family, 33–34, 43;
    sexuality, 42; variations from, 15
Noyes, John Humphrey, 118–119
nuclear family, 2, 11, 15–23,
    24, 26–33, 46, 65, 77; aged,
    43; alternatives to, 42, 45; division
    of labor, 18–33; kibbutz compared,
    127; norms, 33–34, 43; prein-
    dustrial household, 32–33; so-
    cial mobility, 67; transformations
    in, 131–146; see also
    family; household
nursing, 30

Odhnoff, Camilla, 137
office work, 52
Oneida community (N.Y.), 117,
    118–121, 132, 157
opportunity, 58, 62
Origin of the Family, Private Property
    and the State, The (Engels), 124
orphanages, 100–101
Orthodox Jews, 91; see also Jews
Owen, Robert, 113–115, 123
Oxford English Dictionary, xvii

parenting, see child care and rearing
paternalism: preindustrial society,
    9–10, 12; tribal society, 2–3
patriarchy: bourgeois family, 21;
    Hispanics, 85, 86–87; Marxism,
    124–125; parenting, 37;
    preindustrial society, 11; sex role,
    88–89; wages, 23
peer groups, 73

Peirce, Melusina Fay, 121–122, 157
permanence, 48–49
Phalanx (utopia), 116–117
Philadelphia Life Center, 150–151
Plato, xx, 108, 110–112, 155, 157
Poland, 101
polyandry, 3, 15
polygamy, 3–4, 15; Mormons, 118
population changes, 15
Portland State University, 153
poverty: aged, 102; blacks, 86; child
    socialization, 71, 80; defined, 55,
    57; discrimination, 85; divorce,
    95–96; family size, 63, 64;
    household composition, 66–67;
    marriage, 92; self-esteem, 78–79;
    working class, 56–57
primogeniture, 9; see also
    inheritance
Princeton University, 83
private property, 9, 10; see
    also property
production (social): division of labor,
    18; nuclear family, 15–17;
    women's work, 34–35
promiscuity, 112, 118, 126, 152
property: bourgeois family, 20, 21;
    capital formation, 16; Church, 7;
    feudal society, 10; marriage age,
    39; Marxism, 124; nuclear family,
    32; preindustrial household, 9, 14;
    utopias, 119; wages, 31
prostitution, 125
Protestants: family size, 63; marriage,
    91; see also religion

race: child socialization, 82;
    intermarriage, 91; social class
    and, 85; utopias, 115–116; see also
    blacks; Chicanas; Hispanics
Rainbow Community, 155–156
Randall, Margaret, 134
Rappites, 113
recession(s): blacks, 86; social
    mobility, 68; unemployment, 56
Reich, Wilhelm, 117
religion: Catholics, 63, 91; courtly
    love, 7; feudalism, 7–8; Jews, 63,
    91, 125–131; kibbutz movement,

131; Mormons, 117, 118;
Protestants, 63, 91; utopias,
117–121
Republic, The (Plato), 108, 110–111
retirement, 42–43; income, 101–103
Rexed, Bror, 136
Rockefeller, David, 55
Rockefeller family, 55, 65
roles; family definition, xviii; *see
also* sex roles

scientific socialism, 123–125
self-esteem: sex role, 88–89; upper
class, 83–84; working class, 79
serfs, 8–9, 10, 11
serial monogamy, 152
servants: child care, 66, 71;
indentured, 11, 14
sex role: child care, 133–136,
137–140, 142–146; communes,
149–151; division of labor, 36–38,
132–133, 141, 157; kibbutz
movement, 130; More, 111;
nuclear family, 44; Plato, 110;
retirement, 103; socialization in,
70, 82, 88–90; Sweden, 137–138
sexuality: bourgeois family, 21–22;
child socialization, 80–81; communes, 151–152; Fourier, 116,
117; marriage, 95, 97; Marxism,
125; norms, 42; Noyes, 118–119;
Shakers, 117–118
Shakers, 117–118, *128–129*
Shrock, Alice, 143–144
Shrock, Randall, 143–144
single-parent family, *iv,* xvii–xviii,
xix, 34, 77, 109; blacks, 86;
increase in, 64–65; poverty, 57
single-person household, 132;
increase in, 90–91, 97; pros and
cons, 97–98
Skinner, Larraine, 147
slaves and slavery (American), 11,
14, 25, 111, 115–116
social class: aging, 102; categoriza-
tion of, 53–58; child socialization,
71–72; criteria for, 52–53; defined,
50; family and, 15, 50–62, 68; feudalism, 5; lineage, 13; marriage,
91–92, 95–96; Marx, 123–125;

race, 85; subjectivity in, 52;
*see also entries under names
of classes*
socialism, 123–125
socialization, 68–90; defined, 69–70;
middle class, 72–75; sex role, 70,
82, 88–90; social mobility, 69,
72–75; upper class, 81–84;
working class, 78–81
social mobility: discrimination, 84;
family composition, 67–68;
marriage, 55, 92; relativity in,
51–52; socialization, 69, 72–75;
working class, 67, 78–81
social production: division of labor,
18; nuclear family, 15–17;
women's work, 34–35
Social Security, 57, 102; *see also*
retirement
social services, 64; aging, 103; child
socialization, 71, 79; family role
in, xviii; *see also* welfare
Soviet Union, 101
Sparta (ancient), 1, 116
Spock, Benjamin, 75, 145–146
Standard Oil, 55
standards of living, 57–61
sterilization, 40–41; *see also* birth
control
stirpiculture, 119
Supreme Court: New Jersey, 98;
United States, 91
surplus value, 51
Sweden, 133, 157; child care, 35;
family policy, 136–141
Swerdlow, Amy, xvi–xxi, 107–159
Syphax family, 84

Talmon, Yonina, 126
teenage mothers, 64
Tibet, 15
tribal societies: child care, 29;
feudalism and, 5; kinship in, 2–4
Triola, Michelle, 98
Trobriand Islanders, 2–3
Tupi-Kawahib people, 3–4

unemployment, 68; blacks, 86; working class, 56
unions, 52

United Nations, 132
United States Bureau of the Census,
    xviii, 132; family definition, xvi,
    xvii, 47–48, 49
United States Department of Labor,
    57–58
United States Rubber Company, 55
United States Supreme Court, 91
universality, 49
unmarried-couple households, *see*
    cohabitation
upper class: aging, 102; blacks, 84;
    child socialization, 71, 81–84;
    defined, 53, 55; family size, 63;
    household composition, 65–66;
    marriage, 92, 95; *see also*
    social class
upper middle class: aging, 102;
    defined, 53, 55; *see also*
    social class
urbanization, 16
Utopia (More), 111–112
utopias, 107, 108, 158; Campanella,
    112; Fourier, 116–117; Gilman,
    122–123; More, 111–112;
    Mormons, 118; Owen, 113–115;
    Plato, 110–111; Shakers, 117–118;
    Wright, 115–116; *see
    also* communes and communi-
    tarian societies

vassalage, 5–6
Victorianism, 22
Vine, Phyllis, xx, 107–159
violence, 74, 93

wages, 17; aged, 43; blacks, 86;
    Chicanos, 87; child rearing, 40;
    housework, 30–32, 121–122; mar-
    riage age, 39; nuclear family, 44;
    surplus value, 51; unions, 52;
    women, 36–37, 158 (*see also*
    labor force, women in); working

class, 22–23
wealth, 51; *see also* capital; property
Weiss, Michael, 154
welfare, 56–57, 65, 68, 79; *see also*
    social services
wetnurses, 29
Who Will Raise the Children
    (Levine), 142
widows, 97, 98; poverty, 57
wife beating, 93
Womanshare Collective (Grants Pass,
    Oreg.), 153
women: black, 86; bourgeois, 19–20;
    Campanella, 112; division of
    labor, 17, 18–26; family role, 104
    (*see also* sex role); feudal society,
    6; heads of households, 91;
    housework role (*see* housework);
    kibbutz movement, 126, 130;
    labor force, xviii, 34–38, 44, 63,
    94, 109, 131–132; marriage laws,
    94; Marxism, 124–125; nursing
    role, 30; Oneida community,
    120–121; Owen, 114; pensions of,
    102; Plato, 110, 111; preindustrial
    society, 12–13; retirement, 103;
    wages, 158; working class, 26, 57
women's movement: sex role, 20;
    Spock and, 146; *see also* feminism
working class, 24; aging, 102; child
    socialization, 72–75, 78–81;
    defined, 56–57; division of labor,
    32; divorce, 95–96; family budget,
    59; nuclear family, 22–23, 26; sex
    roles, 89–90; social mobility, 67,
    78–81; *see also* social class;
    entries under other classes
World War II, 131
Wright, Frances, 115–116, 158
Wunambal people, 2–3

Yale University, 83
Yugoslavia, 101

A Note on Language

IN EDITING BOOKS, The Feminist Press attempts to eliminate harmful sex and race bias inherent in the language. In order to retain the authenticity of historical and literary documents, however, our policy is to leave their original language unaltered. We recognize that the task of changing language usage is extremely complex and that it will not be easily accomplished. The process is an ongoing one that we share with many others concerned with the relationship between a humane language and a more humane world.